AGH 2780
NDLC / No #

Jan 707
56

ELECTRONIC TRADING

AF768724

ELECTRONIC TRADING

A Practical Handbook

Pete Gardner

BUTTERWORTH
HEINEMANN

Butterworth-Heinemann Ltd
Linacre House, Jordan Hill, Oxford OX2 8DP

A member of the Reed Elsevier group

OXFORD LONDON BOSTON
MUNICH NEW DELHI SINGAPORE SYDNEY
TOKYO TORONTO WELLINGTON

First published 1994

© Pete Gardner 1994

All rights reserved. No part of this publication may be reproduced in any material form (including photocopying or storing in any medium by electronic means and whether or not transiently or incidentally to some other use of this publication) without the written permission of the copyright holder except in accordance with the provisions of the Copyright, Designs and Patents Act 1988 or under the terms of a licence issued by the Copyright Licensing Agency Ltd, 90 Tottenham Court Road, London, England W1P 9HE. Applications for the copyright holder's written permission to reproduce any part of this publication should be addressed to the publishers

TRADEMARKS/REGISTERED TRADEMARKS
Computer hardware and software brand names mentioned in this book are protected by their respective trademarks and are acknowledged.

British Library Cataloguing in Publication Data
A catalogue record for this book is available from the British Library

ISBN 0 7506 1905 8

Typeset by P.K.McBride, Southampton
Printed and bound in Great Britain

Contents

Part 3

"Understanding the real issues and how to overcome them."

Part 4

The future of Electronic Trading

Part 5

Preface

Once upon a time, a young man was installing a new purchasing system and his customer asked him to look at implementing an electronic link to his suppliers whilst the new system was being implemented. No, it's not a fairy tale, the author was that young man and is now considerably older because of it. This rapid ageing process was a result, quite simply, of the author's and the customer's lack of appreciation of the traumatic effect a simple request like that could have on the people involved and the business operation.

Telecommunication networks, together with a variety of techniques for interchanging information can be used to conduct business electronically - or turn a business upside down if you don't implement them in the right way. Our initial venture into electronic links with trading partners was not perfect by a long way, but thankfully, it was sufficiently successful that it generated a corporate ***electronic trading*** (ET) programme aimed at distributing everything except hardware and people electronically - i.e. doing business electronically. As you progress through the book, I hope that the meaning of "*electronic trading*" or "*doing business electronically*" will become clear and you will understand what's involved with this new way of trading. I used a term earlier that you will find throughout the following chapters - "*trading partners*" - these are the people who will be involved (**partners**) in exchanging electronic transactions (**trading**) with you and they may be within your own or in your customer's, supplier's or agent's organisations.

"**Electronic Trading**" has been written to explain what ET is, why businesses need it, who will be involved, how to go about it, and where you should and should not apply these techniques. It is largely based on the "coal-face" experience of the author and other contributors, and if it can help others through the times of frustration, challenge and sheer exhilaration that will arise from trying to implement an ET programme, then it will have been more than worth the effort involved in writing. Don't think that what you are about to read is a blueprint for how we undertook ET in our company, it's not. There's a lot of hindsight been used when writing this, and it's more a case of "this is how we would do it now", given the knowledge we have gained during the past few years.

It isn't intended that the book should be the expert's reference guide to all the various ET technologies and techniques. There are many books on the market that can give you in-depth advice on the specific subject areas - I'll leave it to the experts. The bibliography section lists some of the reference material available that, together with the 'Useful Addresses' section should provide you with the source of a great deal of relevant information, guidance and advice. However, I wouldn't like to think that this book is simply a superficial overview of these subjects, I have tried to concentrate on providing all the relevant information to enable you to ask the right questions. Inevitably, the balance of too much or too little information is difficult to achieve and some readers may find certain sections lacking, whilst others will find some too detailed and if this is the case for you, please let me know.

Wherever possible, I've attempted to incorporate case study material throughout the book in the most appropriate sections and to provide the widest possible scope of examples in terms of both technology and geography. ET however, is still an evolving concept and a large number of the real life examples are of the more mature ET techniques such as electronic mail (E-mail) and electronic data interchange (EDI); in the larger companies and in certain geographical areas (Europe and USA predominantly); but I think I've managed to find some interesting, alternative ones.

The book has been written in plain, non-technological terms wherever practical, because ET is a business issue and the technology needed to facilitate it is relatively straight forward. It's aimed at everyone who needs to be involved with ET: users, business managers at all levels, system procurers, designers and developers, network and infrastructure specialists, and of course your own trading partners. It is hopefully of particular benefit to the poor soul who is responsible for getting the ET programme off the ground - they have the author's sympathy for the times of frustration and hard-work to come - **good luck** and believe me, it will be fun! I've included a glossary at the end of the book, which should provide you with an explanation of all the jargon you are likely to meet along the electronic business highway. It's interesting to note that there are several examples in the Glossary of a single mnemonic having multiple meanings - an indication of the broad scope of ET.

ET is probably one of the fastest growing applications of Information Technology (IT) in today's business world and, where applied correctly, it truly is the exploitation of IT for business gain. ET can bring tremendous benefit to any commercial operation who use it to their advantage and it will then help the business survive in today's increasingly competitive market place.

Don't think that your company or level of business is too small to consider ET, because there are a number of low-cost options available, and remember that it is easier for you to take the initiative than to be driven into ET by one of your trading partners - **"do it unto others before they do it unto you"**. However, remember that trading electronically should be a partnership between organisations where both sides agree the way they will trade, to achieve the 'win-win' situation. You may find though, that the more powerful your trading partner, the more likely it is that they will want to dictate terms to you - so be prepared.

At the time I got involved in ET (in 1987) most, but by no means all staff in our company, were using a proprietary mainframe based E-mail service, our computer terminals were predominantly "dumb" - simple screens and keyboards communicating with remote mainframe computers. Any word-processing tended to be text only and carried out by secretaries on stand-alone Word Processors.

Today, our company has an integrated office system providing E-mail, word processing, spreadsheets, electronic diaries and so on, to the majority of staff; one of the largest X.400 interpersonal mail services in Europe; and also has electronic links to a large number of external trading partners. These facilities have had a tremendous impact on the culture of the company and on activities such as the preparation of this manuscript. Just consider:-

- this book has been word-processed ***by the author***, who now has a PC at home & work and can transfer files between the two.
- it was distributed for comment by electronic mail, saving the printing and photocopying time, cost and effort.
- moved from the word processor to a desk top publishing package to build in the diagrams, saving rework of the manuscript.
- and finally sent to the publishers on diskette for final editing and typesetting without them needing to retype the document.

- a vast improvement in productivity!

But this is not the end. This scenario still has room for improvement - consider the benefits of being able to electronically mail the manuscript to the publisher and then having desk-top video conference links available between the author and the editor to agree final amendments prior to committing to "print" - it could be issued on CD-ROM, if copyright problems permitted.

Anyway, down to business. We'll start this chronicle by examining, in Part 1, the different ways of doing business electronically and what sort of benefits can be gained from it. This will be followed in Part 2 by an explanation of the "blockers" - why ET can be difficult to implement, even with all its benefits. In Part 3, we'll consider the real issues, rather than the "blockers", in detail and look at the ways of overcoming them. Part 4 will focus on new developments and I'll attempt to look forward and see what the future holds. This section may be viewed as speculative, but at least it will leave you with some thought-provoking statements to mull over on the long cold winter's nights when you may be wondering why you ever got involved in all this. The summary in Part 5 will try and provide some conclusions from the whole book and leave you with some points to ponder.

By the end of it all, I hope you'll have a lot of questions, but feel a real excitement and enthusiasm for embarking on an electronic trading programme - if you don't feel this buzz, and the adrenaline rising, then please pass the book to a colleague because without this you'll find it difficult to succeed!

Pete Gardner

Please feel free to feed back any comments on this text - electronically of course!

E-mail addresses:-

X.400:I=AP;S=Gardner;O=ICL;OU1=STE0411;P=ICL;A=GOLD 400;C=GB

Internet:a.p.gardner@ste0411.wins.icl.co.uk

Acknowledgements

I would like to thank the following for their effort in helping pull together this publication:-

- My employers for their understanding whilst I've been working on the project.
- The ICL "Electronic Traders" for their help in reviewing the manuscript, especially Bill Birkett, Steve Davies, Bob Gillies, Andy Gracie, Steve Sharman, Phill Smith, Chris Taper and Mike Warke.
- International Network Services for a large amount of case study material on EDI applications.

Special thanks must go to Phil Bloor at Biddulph High School, without whom this book may never have been written, as he was the one who publicly encouraged me to put metaphorical pen to metaphorical paper, after he spent a week work-shadowing me.

Finally, I would like to thank my long suffering family for putting up with my antisocial working habits and their patience during the time it's taken to write it. Especially my wife, Maura, for accepting that the kitchen and all other jobs "in progress" could wait until after the book - and she's still waiting - maybe I'll finish them after the next one!

Part 1

"What does 'Electronic Trading' actually mean and why do we need it?"

Electronic Trading (ET) is a way of moving towards the once mooted paperless office, or to put it another way, doing business electronically. It's the way of exchanging business transactions electronically, regardless of the type of object that this entails, and it's important to consider this holistic approach rather than simply looking at individual techniques and technologies. After all, when we trade with another individual or organisation, we interchange a variety of information objects (speech, words, pictures, etc.) and looking at ET means that we have to consider all these different forms of interchanges or transactions.

This section will describe the various transaction types and the technologies that can be used to conduct these without paper.

We will also explore the reasons why businesses are looking at this form of trading and what the main benefits are. We will have a brief look at the Management in the Nineties programme and then review the history of electronic trading during this century.

1 What is Electronic Trading?

"This is already my ninth hour at work, and I have not yet eaten or drunk, I have been seated all day without ever going out, and I won't get to eat until night, but who will deliver me from this endless round of letters and invoices? It's my fate always to remain a common scrivener like an old horse in harness.", This quotation is not from someone in our recent past, but from a Florentine Merchant in 1385, and indicates that the need to address the "paper mountain" has been with us for quite a considerable time.

At a Computer Users Association meeting in 1982, it was stated that "The paperless office is as likely as the paperless toilet". However, in the 1990s, the paperless office is not a myth, it's now a reality that can be achieved, albeit with a great deal of careful planning, justification and cultural change. This level of control is essential unless you want to make David Steel's prediction at the 1983 Harrogate Liberal Assembly come true "To err is human - but for a real cock-up you need a computer".

Almost every form of business transaction can be conducted by electronic means, whether:-

- people to people.
- people to/from business system.
- business system to business system.

There are numerous cases of organisations addressing the ever increasing volumes of paper and the problems that this leads to. To take a few examples:-

- In the USA, the M1 tank portable maintenance aid replaces 16,000 pages of manuals and enables diagnostics to be taken in 10-20 minutes rather than days. The F16 fighter portable computer plugs into the plane's electronic data system and ties into a central database, replacing 300 technical manuals and making the plane's maintenance and operational details accessible.

- Internet, the computer communications network established 20 years ago by the US Government for space and military research projects, now has 15 million users working through 3 million workstations on over 10,000 Local Area Networks (LANs) in over 50 countries. Mailbox addresses have already had to be extended to cope with increased usage and they are now adding new facilities such as multimedia and video links. Pipex, the UK Internet agents, report that links to the network are growing by 5% per month and are mainly commercial users.
- A recent survey of 100 European telecommunications managers, carried out by the Yankee Group Europe, indicates that the top two changes for networks over the next 5 years will be LAN installation & interconnection (allowing more people to share information electronically) and bandwidth increase (extending our ability to carry more across the networks).
- Microsoft have just released the "Art Gallery: The Collection of the National Gallery" containing paintings by Van Gogh, Titian, Raphael, Holbein, Rembrandt and Michelangelo, in addition to 5,000 pages of text, 700 artist biographies and a glossary of 500 artistic terms - on CD-ROM. Also available are Multimedia Mozart: The Dissonant Quartet and Multimedia Stravinsky: The Rite of Spring.
- Moscow is to get its first banking Automated Teller Machines.
- The Gartner Group estimate that the Video Conferencing market will grow from $500 million today to $7.5 billion by 1997.

However, there are still some disappointing cases of organisations holding on to the old technology when they should be providing the lead to others. An interesting example of this is, ironically, the organisers of conferences on ET subjects, who continue to demand submissions for presentations on paper!

But before we go any further, let me define what I mean by trading electronically. ET is ***"the communication of ANY object of commercial interchange by electronic means"***. We've seen a few examples above of organisations using some of the techniques to achieve this and we'll discuss more later, but let's first look the various types of "commercial interchange" in a bit more detail:

1.1 People to people

Man has been communicating with man since the beginning of time and has endeavoured to overcome the issues associated with this type of intercourse. Communicating by voice is obviously restricted by distance; by the availability (of both parties); by our ability to interpret the message received; and we have continually looked at ways to overcome these restrictions.

Consider:-

- Smoke signals, jungle drums, Morse code, semaphore, radio, and television - all have been devised to carry information to a recipient who is out of earshot.
- Answering machines avoid availability of both parties being necessary.
- Sign language and translation are used to help the recipient who cannot hear or understand the person delivering the message.

Communicating by the written word has similarly been plagued by these problems, in addition to a further one - media. Even in the earliest days this has tested man's initiative, as stone is a very difficult medium to transport.

But consider:-

- Messengers and postal services carry messages over distance.

- Mail boxes avoid the need for the recipient to be present when the message is delivered.
- Braille and language translation convert the message into a format understandable by the recipient.
- Parchment and then paper replaced the more cumbersome media used in the stone age.

With man's constant need to address these problems, together with the ever decreasing cost of technology and the advances in telecommunication facilities, these forms of interpersonal exchanges can now be improved by electronic equipment:- telephones, answer phones, telex, fax, voice-mail, electronic mail (E-mail), video conferencing, etc. and these technologies continue to become more affordable to a larger population as prices decrease. It is remarkable to note that when radios first came on the market, they cost the equivalent of 8 times the average weekly wage and this is typical of the way prices of electronic devices plummet over time. However, it's also noteworthy that in all the advances in technology, improvements in telephony facilities have been completely overshadowed by the enhancements in data network facilities for computer users. Except for the portable telephone, fax and video conferencing, telephony services are largely unchanged since the 1970s.

Let's consider one of these forms of interpersonal communication in a bit more detail and look at why it would be beneficial for an organisation to use it. Take E-mail as an example:-

- The sender and recipient can process the information on their computer terminals at a time (and sometimes location), which suits themselves.
- They can send complex documents of various types (within limits, but we'll discuss these later).
- The recipient can forward messages and documents to other people.
- Documents can be electronically circulated for approval and update.

However, even E-mail has its limitations and disadvantages that must be taken into account:-

- People can become E-mail bound and stop talking to one another.
- E-mail systems are liable to the junk mail syndrome. It's very easy to indiscriminately copy a large number of people on mail items.

E-mail systems are now extremely prevalent, relatively inexpensive to install and are becoming increasingly more "intelligent" with (for example) filtering mechanisms. They can be used to send internal mail within a company, but are now also being used for communicating with external trading partners. I even noted a job advertisement recently which proposed that applicants should send their CVs by E-mail - it was for an IT position though! Furthermore, E-mail is also an extremelyeffective way of engendering an ET culture.

Figure 1.1-1 shows the way an E-mail system works and how it can be used for internal as well as external communications.

ELECTRONIC MAIL SYSTEM

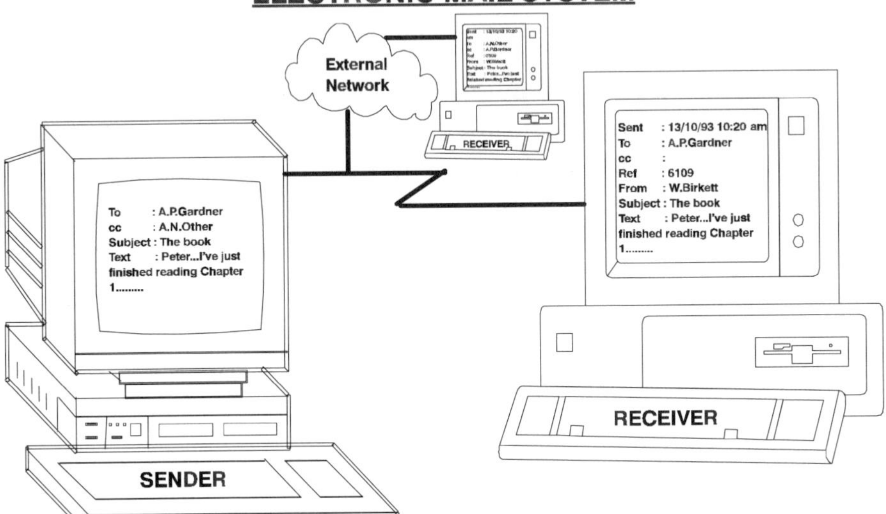

Figure 1.1-1

So what's driving this type of application? There are sound business drivers behind the implementation of these systems - it is estimated that US managers spend anywhere between 30 and 80% of their time in meetings and the Meeting Management Institute of 3M Corporation recently cited one Fortune 500 company that wasted $71 million a year on "bad" meetings, ones that are inconclusive, and they are looking at ways of eliminating face-to-face meetings.

Also, E-mail systems are increasingly becoming integrated with office automation systems, which means that other business objects can be attached to a mail item and transported to the recipient. These objects include:-

- Word processing documents.
- Spreadsheets.
- Diagrams.
- Computer software.

But bear in mind that the recipient must be able to process these objects. For example:-

- If someone attaches a word processing document to a mail item that has been produced using word processing package XYZ then the recipient may have great difficulty reading the document if he does not use the same word processing package, or one that is compatible with package XYZ (see Figure 1.1-2). In this case conversion will be required. This subject will be discussed further in the standard's section.

Furthermore, with the standards being developed for X.400, we now have the ability to attach trade documents to our mail items and hence transmit Orders, Invoices, etc. in machine readable formats, but we will consider this later when we look at Electronic Data Interchange (EDI).

Finally, there are also the "hidden" benefits to using E-mail - in addition to the productivity gains that you would normally expect

ELECTRONIC MAIL PLUS OTHER "OBJECTS"

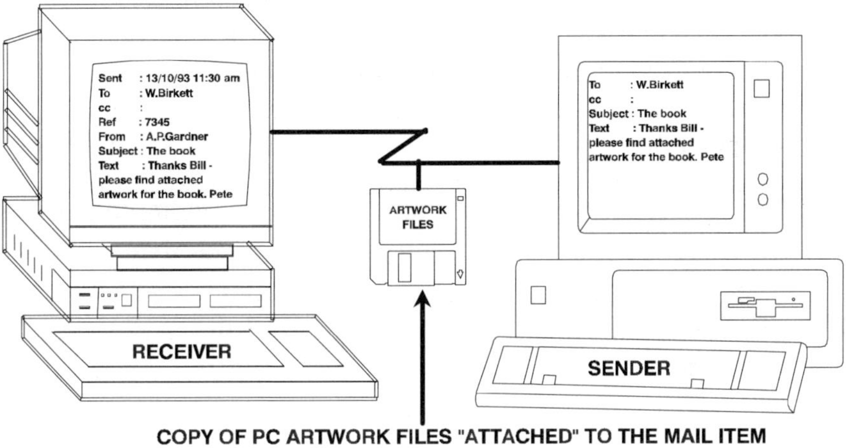

Figure 1.1-2

from this technology, it also allows people to network across organisations and in the current climate of devolution, this can be a tremendous benefit, especially in geographically dispersed organisations.

1.2 People to/from business system

Ever since their introduction, business systems have been producing output which has predominantly been in the form of printed reports, but in recent years, the use of Visual Display Units and Terminals (VDUs and VTs) has become increasingly popular, and remember that we do actually use them in everyday life. For example:-

- Bank automatic cash machines.
- Television teletext services.
- Airport and rail ticket machines.
- etc., etc.

are all forms of computer terminal.

However, even with the advent of this capability, we still insist on maintaining our love of paper or pseudo-paper (e.g. microfiche) when in most cases it's not necessary and is very expensive. With very little change, printed output can be made suitable for viewing on a screen or further processing by computer and then think of all the rain forests and retyping we could save!

Consider:-

- Make reports appropriate for screen viewing (e.g. use 80 columns maximum and portrait rather than landscape format).
- Check what the output will be used for and make sure it's fit for use (e.g. output as a graph or spreadsheet where appropriate).
- Index reports to aid navigation by the user.
- Check what media the customer will accept.

BUSINESS SYSTEM TO PERSON

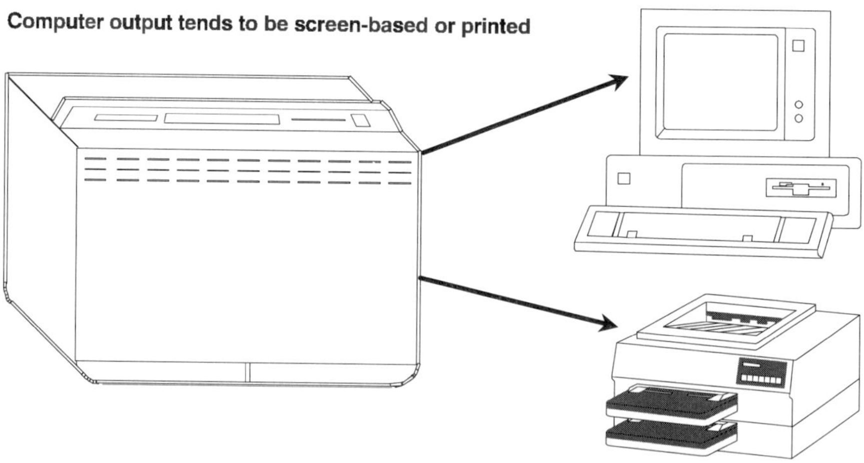

Figure 1.2-1

There are several notable examples of why we should be finding alternatives to paper based information:-

- The documentation carried on the flight deck of a Boeing 747 weighs 70 kg. This prevents the airline carrying 1 extra fare-paying passenger.
- A Health Authority nearly spent £1 million on a building extension to house its increase in medical records, but instead, introduced a Document Image Processing (DIP) system for a fraction of the cost.
- A bank reduced its loan application time from 21 to 7 days by replacing paper with electronic images.
- One optical disk holds the equivalent of 200,000 pages, a juke box of discs can hold the equivalent of 20 million pages of A4 (which would weigh 100 tons and occupy 2 miles of shelf space).
- The National Westminster Bank in the UK is saving £42,000 every year by transferring computer print to screen based reports.

These are impressive facts that can't be ignored when designing systems and choosing the output media for users.

Since the introduction of VTs, input to business systems is now predominantly electronic via one of a number of different types of input devices:- keyboard, mouse or more specialist devices such as bar-code readers, point of sale equipment, scanners, etc. Gone are the days of preparing data on punched cards, paper tape and magnetic tape for subsequent input to the system. There are countless examples of the application of these specialist devices. Just consider the advances made by the retail industry in capturing information at point of sale and Westminster Council in London, who equipped its 200 traffic wardens with hand-held terminals, to replace manually produced, parking tickets.

There are also some cases of these devices now being used in industries where one wouldn't necessarily expect to come across them and a more noteworthy one I came across recently was the use of bar-code readers to help record and combat cattle disease in Holland's 5 million cow population.

Although improvements continue to be made in these input mechanisms (e.g. voice and hand-writing recognition - *cf.* Apple Computers' Newton Messaging Pad), the point very often overlooked is that a great deal of input to systems is actually output from another one. We should always investigate whether the information to be input to the system can be captured and processed electronically, not just input more efficiently. What's the point of providing someone with a report, if what they really want to do is input the information into a PC spreadsheet, we may as well provide them with the spreadsheet.

Access to External Information

If we extend the scope of this section a little further, we start to consider accessing information that is held in systems outside the control of our own organisation. In the majority of cases, to gain access to this information, you will normally need to contact the organisation who holds the information and request the details you need. So the real users of our systems may be in a different organisation or company to the system itself.

Some organisations have now started to address this, but it's only the tip of the iceberg - we have a great potential to save a lot of time and effort by opening up our systems to not only our own organisations, but also to external trading partners. This obviously demands that we must consider the security and auditability of access from external parties, but the travel companies have done it and companies like Thomas Cook allow travel agents to book holidays on-line from their own offices. With appropriate security provisions, certain users can view seats that are not yet booked, whilst other, more privileged, users can reserve unused seats. Why distribute information when all that is needed is access to it?

Unfortunately, one of our biggest burdens is the legacy systems developed during the last twenty years, that have predominantly been designed for internal business users with little or no consideration having been given to access from outside the immediate organisation. This is now starting to change, as

PERSON TO BUSINESS SYSTEM

The majority of computer input is done using the keyboard or the mouse

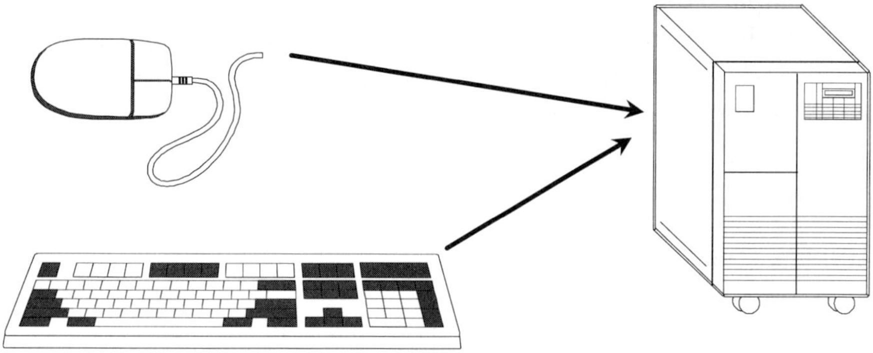

Figure 1.2-2

businesses are looking more and more at their trading partners (customers, suppliers, agents, etc.) as an integral part of their commercial operations. Business systems need to be designed to consider input, output and even updating by internal **and** external users, with the minimum of re-inputting. However, don't forget that the burden of our legacy systems will not go away until they are replaced by systems designed for tomorrow's business.

Furthermore, the change needed in our system design must start at the time when requirements for new systems are defined, and business managers should be insisting on electronic input and output from systems and trading partners. System developers should be thinking about open system architecture in terms of "information seekers" - the people and organisations who need information from the system - and not just in terms of hardware and software interworking. Figure 1.2-3 indicates the sort of architecture that is needed for the customer-oriented system of the future and we'll discuss this further in Part 3.

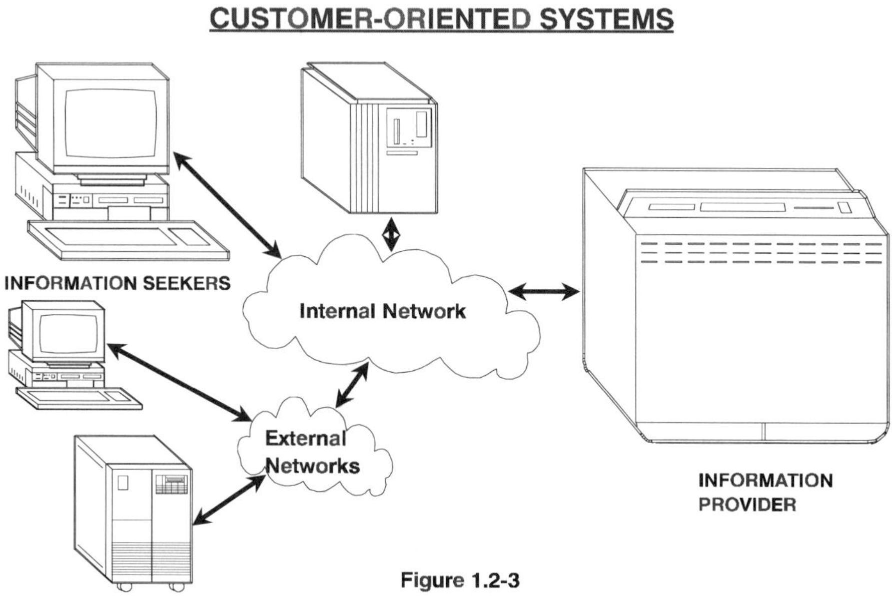

Figure 1.2-3

Each information seeker will have potentially different requirements on the information provider, but the system should be constructed so that the component that controls access to information should be able to cope with all the requirements. After all, if you can service an external customer's information needs in this way, then the savings within your company are tremendous and it can promote a very good image to your customer.

Another form of people-to-system communication is in the area of remote computer diagnostics and system management. In the early days of computers, if the machine became faulty, the customer rang his supplier who sent an engineer to the customer site to investigate and hopefully fix the fault. For a number of years now, remote system diagnostics have become widely used allowing the engineer to access the customer's machine from the supplier's site and hence the engineer only needs to travel to the customer site if a replacement part needs to be fitted. This has not only reduced the time to fix the fault, but has also reduced the cost of repair by cutting out unnecessary travel, in the cases where a replacement part is not needed.

Similarly, it's now possible to manage a complete computer system remotely, removing the need for systems support staff to be physically near the machines being managed and allowing them to support multiple systems from a single site - the "lights out" computing scenario. Also, systems can now proactively support themselves, electronically informing the support staff when things are starting to go wrong or even sometimes before they go wrong.

Integrated Office Equipment

The last area I want to cover in this section is the integration of office equipment. Already we've seen how we can "talk" to computer systems using a variety of devices, but with developments underway currently, we will soon be able to "talk" to office equipment in a similar way. Within a number of companies, it is now possible to send a Fax from your office system just as you would send an E-mail, and Microsoft and Rank Xerox for example, are working on the integration of PCs to photocopiers. The level of sophistication of the office systems available to us will continue to increase over the next decade, giving us more and more capability to distribute everything electronically.

1.3 Business system to business system

It is a widely held belief that over 70% of all computer output is re-input to another computer system. This is indeed a sad indictment of the way we have failed to exploit computer power. In the 1970s and 1980s, the problem was standards, but organisations like the trade facilitation boards have done some sterling work in the field of defining common standards for commercially traded documents e.g. orders and invoices.

This work resulted firstly in national standards for electronic data interchange (EDI) (e.g. ANSI X.12 in the USA and TRADACOMS in the UK) and more recently International standards (EDIFACT). EDIFACT (EDI For Administration, Commerce and Transport) can be said to be succeeding where Esperanto failed - we have a common language for conducting business.

So for commercial trade documents, we have no excuse for arguing that ET is not possible because of standards or technology. We have the document standards and as we will discuss later, there are various ways of forging the communication links between computers. However, let's not dwell on the technology at this point as we will explore it in more detail in Part 3 - suffice it to say that it is not a major issue.

Fine, we have established that commercially traded documents can be easily communicated electronically, but what about all the other forms of trading "objects" that we want to exchange with our trading partners? e.g.

- drawings
- letters
- pictures
- money

Any one of these can be exchanged between companies assuming that the form of the communication is agreed and understood by both parties. Just as we have standards for commercial documents, we need standards for other forms of "documents". Although in a number of cases (e.g. drawings) there is not yet an agreed international standard, there are a number of different local, national and industry standards that can be used (e.g. IGES, SGML), so interchange of these items is possible. However, some of these standards are not widely used because of their proprietary or national heritage and the risk is that you may have to change horses if you choose the wrong one, but if your systems are designed with this consideration in mind, the change should be minimal - we will look at this issue further in Part 3.

The major consideration for this aspect of ET is that computer output sent electronically to another system should be capable of being processed by the receiving systems - not just received by it. The receiving system should not need human intervention to enable processing of the information to take place. Take for example the work that has been done by Eurodollar and HPI (a vehicle information specialist). To overcome the problem that 1 in 70 rental cars are stolen in the UK, Eurodollar now log all car details electronically with HPI who provide a service to car dealers to allow them to check the details of cars being offered for sales and hence identify stolen rental cars - 8,000 alerts a year are now raised as a result of this application of ET.

Figure 1.3-1 shows an example of system to system interworking.

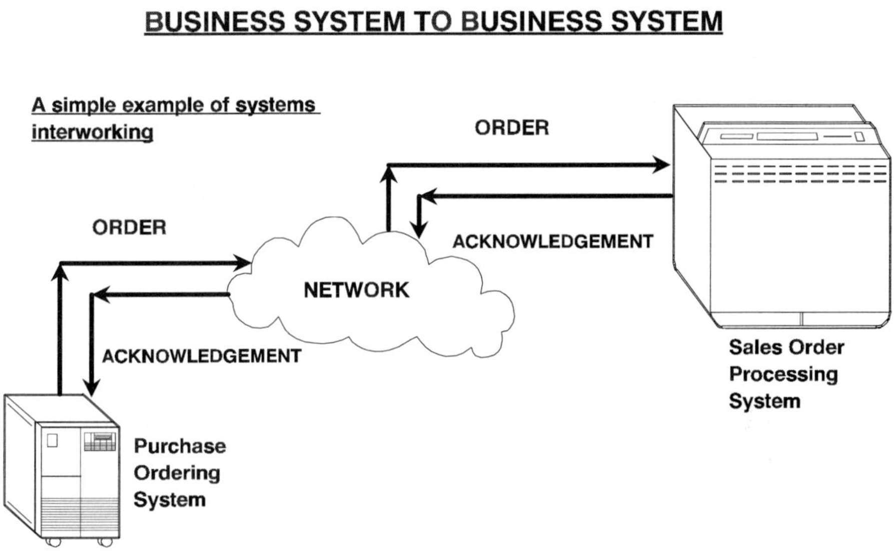

Figure 1.3-1

As I mentioned earlier, we must start recognising when a transaction is capable of being system to system, as there are a number of instances of systems interworking with people where the person involved is purely an intermediary, simply adding cost and increasing the risk of errors being generated. Figure 1.3-2 gives an example of this.

One last area to consider before we leave this section, is system to machine interface and we briefly touched upon this earlier when we looked at the developments in office integration. However, there is another aspect of this subject that has been in use for some time - machine control - and certainly in the

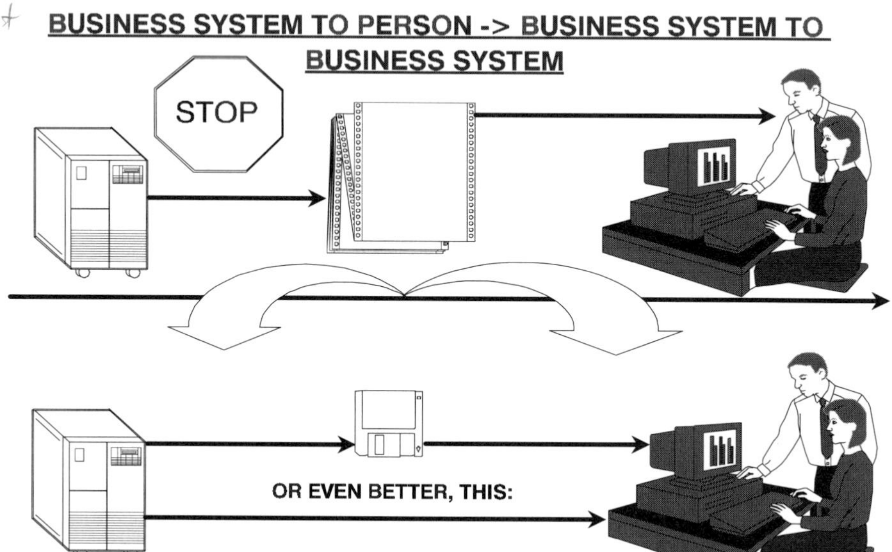

Figure 1.3-2

manufacturing industry, control of automatic store pickers and AGVs (automated goods vehicles) has been prevalent for some time. This type of system to system communication is what is driving the ever increasing application of machine automation.

1.4 Summary

One important aspect of all these forms of ET is that they need standards, both for the information being sent and for the method of transporting the information, but this is no different to more "conventional" forms of trading - for example our postal service (or snail mail):-

If we want to send a letter to a foreign country, we need to consider:-

- If we write in a particular language, will the recipient be able to understand it?
- If the recipient can't understand the particular language, will they be able to get the letter translated?
- Do we need to write the letter in the recipient's language or

an alternative one understandable by both parties (a common standard)?

- Will the address, in the form we write it, be understandable to the postal delivery service and thus get delivered to the right address?

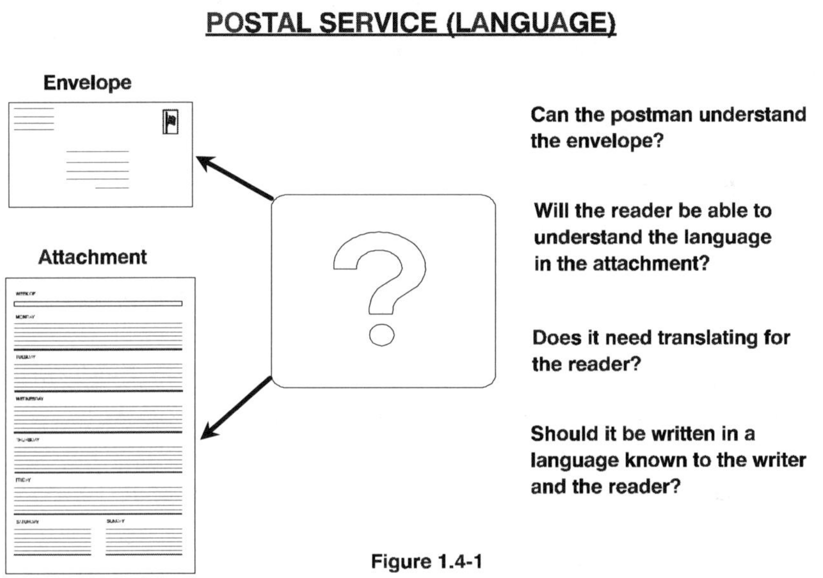

Figure 1.4-1

Secondly, we need to consider the transportation of the letter:-

- Is there a postal service to the recipient's address?
- How long will it take to get there and hence when do we need to post it? Do we need to send it airmail?
- What value stamp do we need to put on the letter?
- Do we need to send it recorded delivery to ensure it gets there?

So the postal service is in reality no different from an electronic system, we still need to consider the document standards for the letter (language) and the transport mechanism to use (surface/air mail, recorded delivery, availability of service to recipient, etc.).

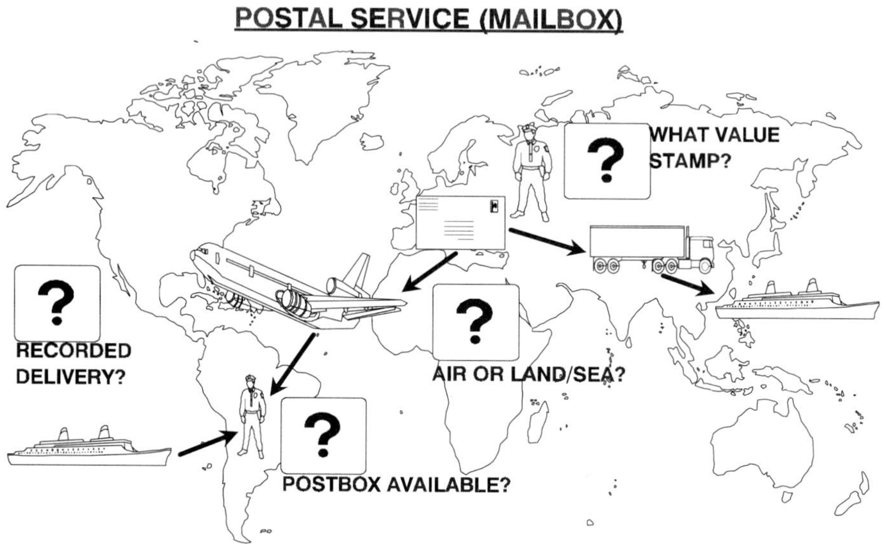

Figure 1.4-2

Also, driven by our own needs, we have already made great strides towards electronic trading in our everyday lives:-

- Fax and telephone answering machines are prolific even for personal use.
- Teletext services and cash machines are now part of normal life.

So let's not say that ET is too difficult and doesn't involve us - we're already using it! If we can adapt so well in our personal lives, what's stopping us from exploiting the techniques for the advantage of our businesses?

Most of the topics we have discussed in this section are representative of commonly available techniques in use today, but there are a number of innovative systems being developed currently which I will try and mention in the appropriate parts of this book. However a couple which immediately spring to mind and are worth mentioning at this point are:-

- Predictive dialling systems are being introduced to aid debt collection. The system logs how many debt collectors are using the system, duration of the telephone calls and the rate at which they are being answered. It then makes predictions based on work patterns, dials the debtor's telephone number and presents the collector with the relevant information on screen to proceed withthe call. This increases the productivity of the collector by between 200 and 400 per cent and normally pays for itself within 1 year.

- The use of multimedia technologies to provide computer based training within traditional educational establishments. Cartoon characters are very strong persuaders when considering educating youngsters and also, if it's on a screen it must be true and worth remembering.
- AMEDIS (Amusement Machine Electronic Data Interchange Standards) application of ET for controlling some 10,000 amusement machines in the UK.
- Geographical Information Systems (GIS) are being used within public utility companies and local government, and have potential for use in vehicle tracking, the military, transport, communications and the emergency, postal and delivery services - the computerised map.
- "Seeing chips" of the future will provide applications in vehicles (e.g. "intelligent" driving mirrors) and fingerprint, face and text recognition systems.

Some people will argue that these examples are not "trading" (and hence ET), but trading must be considered in its most catholic meaning. The storage of information electronically and subsequently making it available to a person or another system is a form of trading - (electronic) information trading.

If I can leave you with one simple message from this chapter, it's:- think laterally when considering ET, there's more to this subject than EDI and E-mail, networks and computer systems. The more holistic approach to this subject holds far more potential than concentrating on specific areas.

Think Electronic!

2 The Potential Benefits

Figure 2-1

Figure 2-1 shows ICL's commitment to trading electronically, but as with any other business programme, there need to be quantifiable benefits for an ET programme to be viable, otherwise why should we even bother doing it? I wouldn't say that ICL has been perfect in measuring every benefit gained from ET, but they can prove it has been worthwhile.

2.1 Tangible Benefits

There are different categories of benefits from any business programme, Firstly, there are the obvious and tangible ones that can be achieved by improving the commercial processes. Distributing business objects electronically rather than manually is just one way of improving a process:-

- Reduction in the transaction cycle time. It is far quicker to communicate electronically than by traditional paper means, especially for trading partners who are large distances apart.
- Improved accuracy through eradication of rekeying. If the transaction is received and processed electronically then fewer errors should occur.
- Lower cost per business transaction. The cost of creating, handling and processing paper documents can be reduced substantially by electronic communications once the initial development costs have been paid off.

An example of this type of benefit can be seen in the Retail industry, where ET has been used to ensure that perishable produce on its shelves is as fresh as possible by continuously reducing the supply chain cycle times.

2.2 Indirect Benefits

However, in addition to these obvious benefits, there are the more indirect and sometimes intangible ones. For example:-

- Reduced inventory and obsolescence, brought about by the ability to order later, with more accuracy and less forward forecasting, because the order cycle time has been reduced.
- Improved responsiveness of the business because of the increased efficiency of business transactions.
- Higher productivity of staff who do not need to correct errors caused by traditional rekeying of information.
- Enhanced integrity of business information by building auditable electronic business networks.
- Eradication of some of the issues associated with inter working between time zones and geographical areas.
- Closer working relationships with trading partners, more trust and hence earlier joint consideration of opportunities and problems, and easier to do business with.
- Exploitation of new business opportunities and markets.

These benefits are very often quantifiable even though it may be difficult, take for example the New York Mercantile Exchange's (NYREX) 24-hour electronic trading system for energy futures. The Gulf War air strike happened at 19:00 New York time and by the time the market reopened, crude oil had changed price by $8 a barrel - i.e. business doesn't stop just because people in different parts of the world are asleep. A 24-hour electronic trading system allows business to continue even when the normal trading markets "sleep" and helps overcome the problems of geography and time zones.

2.3 The Benefits of Less Paper

There is then a third level of benefits, which are extremely obscure but nonetheless relevant. I would suspect that some of these would probably make even your Chairman break into a smile:-

- Reduction in fire insurance through not maintaining the same volume of paper on company sites.
- Less office space needed due to the reduction in paper storage.

These may seem a bit extreme, but if you consider that before they adopted ET, Marks & Spencer's estimated that they were using 19 ***miles*** of paper each ***week***, then maybe these benefits shouldn't be taken too lightly.

Whatever you select as the benefits to be gained from this method of trading, and there is no generic set, you do need to be able to define a business case. Also remember to ensure that you measure the processes BEFORE and AFTER ET; then you can prove the benefit claims at least in the longer term i.e. once the development costs have been covered.

We will look more closely at the problems of putting a business case together for ET in Part 3, but I've tried to include a number of examples showing how benefit is being obtained within certain organisations, throughout the book.

It is worth noting though, before we end this section, that ET is not something that happens overnight - it's a long term programme and as you read on I'll try and explain some of the reasons for this. Sir John Harvey-Jones MBE recently stated at an ET conference that he's been amazed at how slowly Electronic Trading, in all its forms, and all its ramifications, has actually taken on and spread. I hope by the end of the book you will have a better understanding of the reasons for this.

Understand your business drivers, what benefits you want from ET and how you are going to measure them.

3 Management in the Nineties

The MIT90s programme ('Management In The Nineties Research Programme') was initiated in the mid-1980s by the Sloane School of Management of the Massachusetts Institute of Technology, in response to the turbulence observed in the business environment during the early 1980s. This turbulence was being caused not only by the ever increasing competitiveness in the commercial world and hence the need to constantly improve productivity and effectiveness, but also by continual advances made in technology (electronics, computing and manufacturing), economic systems and new business methods. This turbulence still exists in the 1990s and, if anything, is getting stronger.

The objective of the MIT90s programme was "To develop a better understanding of the managerial issues of the 1990s and how to deal most effectively with them, particularly as these issues revolve around anticipated advances in Information Technology".

The Programme ran for five years and involved:-

- 40 members of the MIT faculty
- 6 members of faculties from other institutions
- 6 research staff and 8 visiting researchers
- 32 research projects
- 80 working papers
- 24 seminars and workshops
- 50 noontime research seminars

and the 12 sponsoring organisations:-

- American Express Company.
- Arthur Young and Company (now Ernst and Young).

- British Petroleum Company plc.
- BellSouth Corporation.
- CIGNA Corporation.
- Digital Equipment Corporation.
- Eastman Kodak Company.
- General Motors Corporation.
- International Computers Ltd.
- MCI Communications Corporation.
- United States Department of the Army.
- United States Internal Revenue Service.

3.1 Recommendations

This group of eminent researchers, institutions and businesses documented a number of findings for the business operation of the 1990s. They recommended:-

- Rethink the core of your business operation.
- Integrate with trading partners for effectiveness.
- Create flexible networked organisations.
- Data and information can be a problem area.
- Educate and train for continuing business change.
- Business managers must be agents of change.

Further details of the findings of this programme can be found in "The Corporation of the 1990s" by Michael Scott Morton.

I trust that you will agree when I say that it is evident from this list, that the application of ET has a major part to play in the MIT90s' approach to business. The whole concept of ET is based on a ***flexible networked organisation*** that allows a company to ***rethink the core of its business operations*** and ***integrate its business operation with that of its trading partners***.

With ET, we can help alleviate the ***data and information problem areas*** by eliminating the need to rekey data and by opening up our systems to provide the right information, to the right people, at the right time. However, to make ET work in any organisation, businesses must ***educate and train for continuing business change*** and ***business managers must be the agents of change***. Hence I believe that the MIT90s study underwrote the need for businesses to take ET seriously as **the** way to do business if they want to remain competitive.

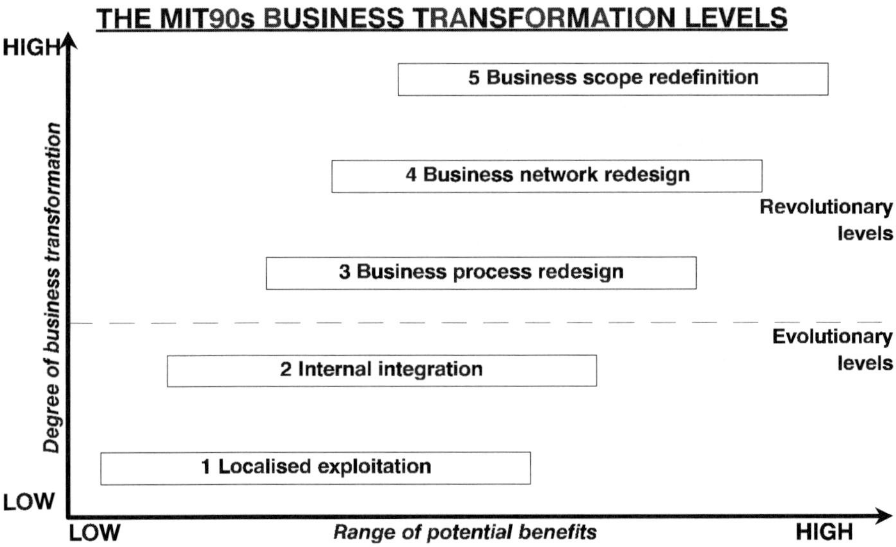

Figure 3-1

Figure 3-1 indicates the different levels of change and the resultant effect on a company, as defined by the MIT90s programme report.

3.2 MIT90s Research in Practice

There are a large number of examples of companies adopting the findings of MIT90s and benefiting from this approach, but I have just included a selection below:-

- The US-owned company Johnson Controls is using EDI to integrate its thirty European sites to form a flexible networked organisation.
- Her Majesty's Stationary Office (HMSO) in the UK states that EDI doesn't make a bad company good, but it does make good companies better.
- Tesco the UK supermarket giant quotes the MIT90s model as an illustration of its approach to exploitation of IT and ET in particular. Tesco now offers its customers cash point facilities by exploiting the facilities of its EPOS tills.
- ICL has changed its core business from computer hardware supply to IT solutions, software and service provision, and has also set up a joint venture company (INS) with GEIS to provide EDI products and services in the UK.
- The US Internal Revenue operation offers its customers the ability to submit tax returns electronically and this is being further exploited by the tax preparers.

The list is endless, but remember that the levels of change indicated by MIT90s (see Figure 3-1) become progressively more difficult to achieve and it is extremely difficult to progress beyond level 2. Unfortunately, this is where the majority of the key benefits are.

Don't expect all the answers from MIT90s, it only tells you what to do, not how to do it.

4 A brief history

We've now looked at what ET is, the different ways we can conduct business electronically and why we should be doing it, but where and how did it all start?

4.1 In the Beginning

As long ago as 1935, Siemens were using a global communications network for internal Telex traffic (i.e. a single user network). Then in the late 1950s, other large companies such as British Airways followed suit but with the involvement of other companies (i.e. multi-user network). The airlines obviously recognised the advantages of global networks and in the 1960s, airline reservation systems became a reality. There were other simpler forms of ET, like the interchange of punched cards, paper and magnetic tape; although these are only limited electronic trading techniques, they are forms of paperless trading.

Also during the 1960s, organisations started to use computer bureau services rather than have their own systems and information was passed to the bureau on either card or tape media or direct via computer terminals connected to the bureau machine. However, all these different ways of trying to improve the efficiency of trading were dogged by problems with the format of the information being exchanged and this brought about the need for companies to look at standards for interchanging information. Systems like BACS (Banker's Automated Clearing System) and LACES (London Airport Cargo Export Scheme) began to emerge once these standards were defined.

Throughout the 1970s, advances in the technology of telecommunication services brought about an upsurge in on-line computer systems and users became accustomed to receiving information when and where they wanted it, without the need to go through the traditional data preparation loop. By the late 1970s, data held within computer systems was starting to be unlocked and used as information at people's desks, without the need to look through vast printed reports. Even though these early attempts at delivery information to the desktop were relatively crude, they did actually deliver benefit to the end users, no matter how limited this was.

4.2 The Need for Standards

In the 1980s, other forms of electronic communication started to emerge (e.g. Electronic Mail, remote machine diagnostics), and, as an example, in 1982 ICL had 200 E-mail users which rose to 12,000 by 1988. However, there was a greater and greater need for national and industry standards and in the mid-1980s, as a result of work done by organisations like the Article Numbering Association (ANA) and the Simpler Trade Procedures Board (SITPRO), open networks for controlling the exchange of Electronic Data Interchange (EDI) transactions were established. These "Value Added" networks (e.g. INS's TRADANET in the UK and GEIS's global EDI*EXPRESS) made it possible for

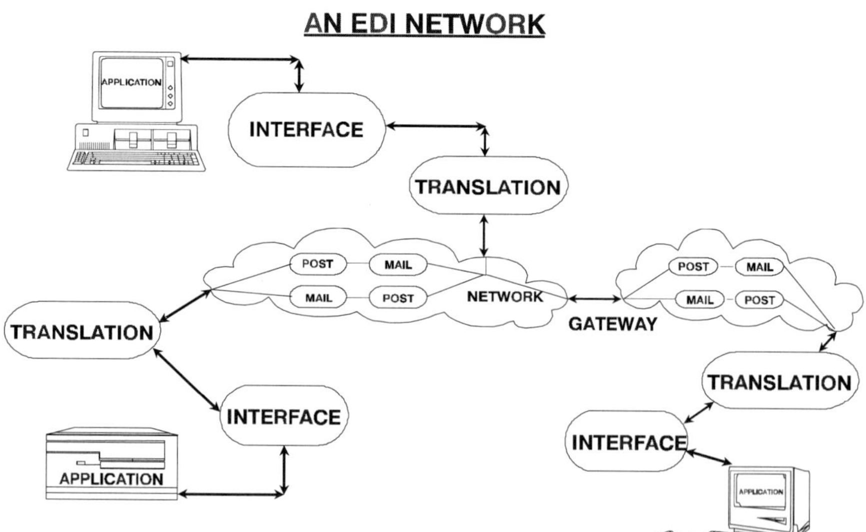

Figure 4-1

companies with incompatible computer hardware to communicate with each other i.e. they were true open system networks. Figure 4-1 shows how a typical EDI network operates.

In addition to the advances made in the methods of transportation of information during this decade, legislation changes and further moves in standards' definition also had a major impact on our ability to trade electronically. In the UK in 1980, a major breakthrough came when the Finance Act allowed Value Added Tax (VAT) invoices to be exchanged electronically between organisations. Then in the late-1980s, the drive towards international standardisation of trade information took over from the limited national and industry ones. A number of messages were defined for the communication of business information (i.e. the EDIFACT EDI standard) and the definition of international standards for a wide range of commercial documents gained momentum.

Figure 4-2 shows the migration from proprietary to, initially, national and then to international standards for trade documents.

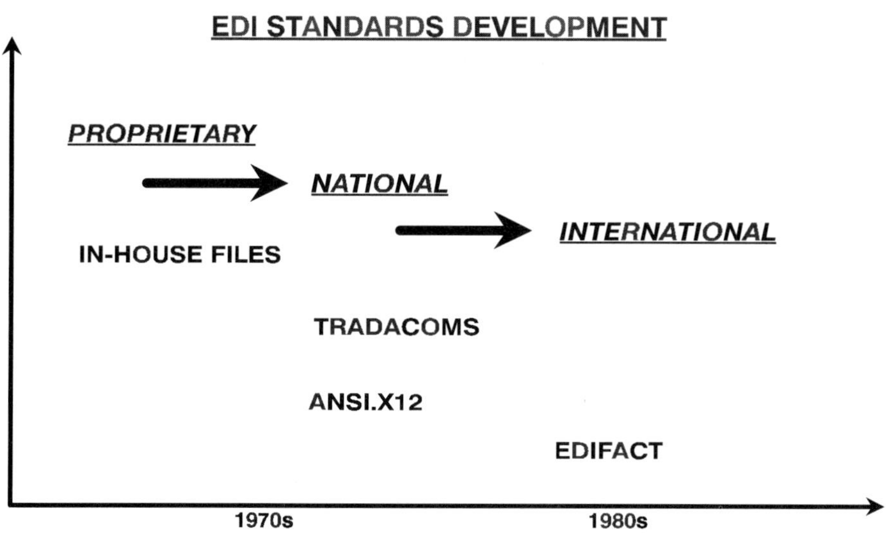

Figure 4-2

Also during the 1980s, International standards for telecommunications were established, and instances of these like the X.400 message handling (transport) protocol together with the X.500 directory (addressing) standard, give us the means to develop open, electronic, business networks for communication with our trading partners. ICL first started using X.400 for interpersonal mail in 1988 and had just 100 users; today it has one of the largest internal X.400 services in Europe with some 27,000 users world-wide. Figure 4-3 shows the growth in E-mail usage in ICL and the transition from proprietary systems to X.400 based services.

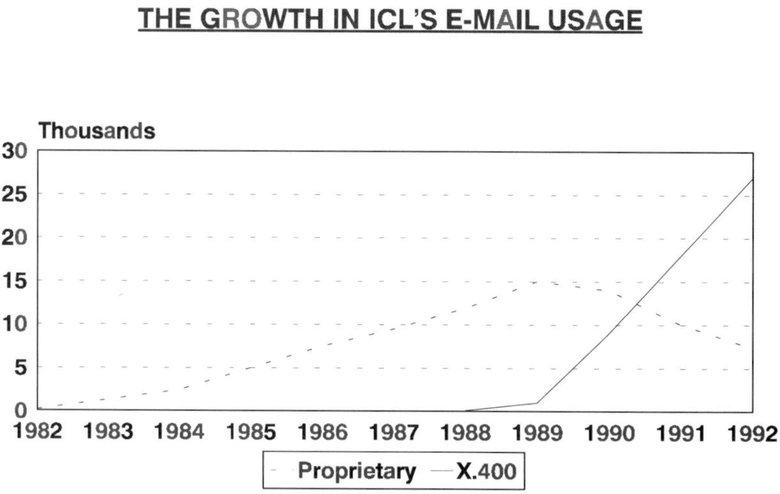

Figure 4-3

The sole driving force for this rapid development in standardising business communications has been the need to improve business efficiency and effectiveness. This drive is unlikely to diminish in the future, as we discussed in the previous chapter on the MIT90s programme, and hence the momentum behind the standards movement can only increase.

In order to continue progress towards easy electronic trading we still need more international standards for items of commercial dealings other than trade documents (pictures, text, etc.). We need improved network interconnection to allow us to trade any business objects through a simple, single network interface and we also need software capable of allowing us to conduct business electronically.

4.3 CALS

However, in the area of standards for business objects, the US Department of Defense's (DoD) ET programme CALS (Computer-aided Acquisition and Logistics Support) looks set to address a large number of the issues. Moreover, I believe that CALS is likely to impact all of us who are trying to implement ET techniques and not just in the standards area, so before we leave this section, I would just like to expand on this thinking in a bit more detail.

CALS was initially conceived to replace the DoD's paper intensive information systems with a totally electronic operation. Now, however, the key strategy is one of setting standards to enable this electronic operation to become a reality. The scope of CALS covers the entire end-to-end manufacturing lifecycle: product design, development, product acquisition (involving sub-contractors and suppliers) and product distribution, operation and support (involving agents and customers).

CALS, I believe, has two major implications for ET: standards and the effect on organisations outside the defence industry. The standards defined as a result of CALS will undoubtedly be ratified by the International Standards Organisation (ISO) and hence have an impact on any organisation interested in distributing information electronically. As companies directly involved with the US DoD start to commit to trading by the CALS mandated standards and methods, they will by necessity start to similarly mandate these practices on their trading partners. These trading partners may be completely outside the defence industry, who will in turn mandate the practices on their trading partners - and on it goes. You can see how the impact of CALS may grow. I will refer more to specific CALS initiatives in the relevant sections, because of this significance to anyone contemplating ET programmes.

4.4 The Present

The 1990s have already started with a rush of new technologies in telecommunications, desktop systems and distributed business applications. The talk is of downsizing and rightsizing, but the major impact will be the growth in the amount of information being distributed electronically within our organisations. I'll not dwell on this any more for the moment, but we'll be looking into the crystal ball later on, and let me just leave you with a simple thought here. The speed of change is continually increasing and unless you are intending to act like the proverbial ostrich and potentially end up like Charles Handy's boiled frog, you need to at the very least be clear about what YOU are going to do about ET. It won't happen by itself, but it may be forced on you if you choose to ignore it. So ***"go for IT"***.

All this has happened in less than a generation - where will we be after the next generation? The rate of change is increasing not decreasing.

Part 2

"If electronic business is that beneficial, why is it so difficult?"

In Part 1, we examined what Electronic Trading (ET) meant, why we should be doing it and the benefits that can be gained from adopting it. I hope that it's now obvious that this method of doing business can be extremely effective for any organisation and that in essence it's not very different in concept from paper-based business. However, it's potentially much more powerful and enables us to improve our business processes and hence efficiency. Why then, if it's so good for us, is it so difficult to implement?

In this section, we will look at the perceived "blockers" before examining the real issues and the ways to address them in Part 3. ET has been the subject of some wildly exaggerated claims of growth and the following chapter should help to explain some of the reasons why the growth has not been as meteoric as the predictions. However, don't view this failure to meet the growth predictions as a reasonable excuse for not embarking on the ET road - this is like burying your head in the sand.

Albert Einstein once said "I never think of the future - it comes soon enough" - we can't afford this luxury, we need to plan our future. The failure in growth rate is a result of the "blockers" put in our way and the complexity that all the seers failed to see. There are still a vast number of sceptics and Luddites around who believe in the old theory that "if God had meant for man to compute he would have given him 10,000 fingers".

The only thing that is certain about the future is that it will be different and we better start planning how we can exploit techniques such as ET to allow us to shape this uncertainty.

5 The blockers

The following pages discuss some of the well-known reasons for not trading electronically. All these, I would propose, are excuses and not valid arguments against ET - these are the ***"blockers"***. However, you must be aware of them and prepared to proffer the counter arguments, if you want to stop them inhibiting your drive towards ET.

THE ET BLOCKERS

Figure 5-1

5.1 People Love Paper

This statement appears to be patently obvious in today's business world and is one of the basic issues when trying to implement ET - but how true is it? The American Declaration of Independence is contained in the equivalent of 3 sides of A4 paper, whereas the EC directive governing the importation of caramel is 22,000 words long (well in excess of fifty pages).

This would seem to indicate that the theory is true, but let's take an example from our own everyday lives, the automatic bank cash machines - how many people ask for a receipt when drawing cash from an Automated Teller Machine (ATM)? The truth is that a great majority of us do (and yes I am one of them), so let's try and understand why. I would suggest that the reasons for doing so are:-

- proof of withdrawal - i.e. we don't trust the banks.
- the need for confirmation that the transaction is OK.
- auditability.

In the case of the first reason, how many times have we known errors occurring in our transactions - i.e. we withdraw £20 and the bank statement shows £30? Furthermore, if the bank statement showed a withdrawal that we hadn't made, would the bank accept the lack of an ATM receipt as proof that we didn't draw cash on a particular day? This suggests that the ATM receipt is only valid as proof of withdrawal when the amount shown on a bank statement disagrees with the actual amount drawn and the instances of this happening are very rare.

Considering the second reason, why should we want confirmation that the transaction was OK when the real proof is whether we get the cash or not? At the moment, this is an emotive issue, open to interpretation and subject to litigation in the UK, but it will undoubtedly be resolved.

So that leaves us with the last point, which I would propose is the only valid one - we want some form of audit trail so that we can either enter it on to our record of running balance in our cheque books or check it against the next bank statement.

Therefore, if the bank could provide us with some form of electronic audit trail, we could probably eliminate the need for ATM receipts on paper. This concept has recently been adopted by some of the fuel companies. Instead of providing saver stamps or vouchers as fuel sales incentives, they now issue an electronic points card which is then updated when you purchase fuel and once filled can be exchanged for money or gifts.

So the real answer to this blocker is to examine what purpose the paper part of a transaction is serving and ensure that the electronic transaction takes this into account.

5.2 Paper is Easier to Use

This is a sad indictment of the way we currently develop our systems. We continue to define system requirements around paper-based processes and hence the results are applications that are designed for document input and output. Living proof of this was my receipt of paper, annotated copies of this manuscript back from the reviewers. I had issued the copy for review electronically, but because of the limitations of current technology, reviewers found it easier to print the document, add their comments and post it back to me using surface mail.

However, if we start by assuming that all input and output from our systems will be electronic AND defining our requirements accordingly, then the systems developed will need to be designed for the ET scenario. Let me give you an example:-

A couple of years ago, I was asked to take responsibility for our Capital Approval Process - a process that ensured that all IT equipment to be purchased was approved by the correct people. The process relied on six levels of signatory from the manager of the person who raised the purchase request, right up to a senior Director.

When I took the process over, it was taking approximately 6 weeks from raising the purchase request to gaining final approval, because the people involved were geographically dispersed and a paper document had to be sent from one signatory to the next using surface mail. Needless to say, I decided that this was:

A) an unacceptable time period and

B) a time consuming, and hence expensive, process to administer and monitor.

The other irony in this paper-based process was that the capital purchase requests were all electronic documents at source.

To solve the problem, I simply insisted that all further requests were to be submitted electronically using our internal E-mail system and that each signatory returned the document to me when he/she had approved it. I or one of my people then simply forwarded it to the next signatory in the chain. This resulted in:

A) an approval time of 4 days on average,

B) I always knew who had the document for approval at any particular time,

C) a fully auditable system and

D) no PAPER!

The only difficulty I had was persuading people that for this particular process, I didn't need a physical signature on a piece of paper to prove authorisation - the proof was the receipt of the document from the authoriser's electronic mailbox.

5.3 People Don't Like Change

It's true that we don't like change, but only when it's uncontrolled or badly implemented. The majority of us thrive on well-controlled change as it can relieve the boredom that results from repetition in all aspects of life. I was amazed recently by an article in an IT publication that questioned the need for standards and advocated the use of proprietary formats for short-term cost and expediency - this person must really have had his fingers burnt trying to use standards - but I would urge you all to question this sort of short-sighted advice.

Let's look again at our personal finances and see how change has come about here. Not many years ago we all used cash and nothing else because there wasn't an alternative. Then came cheque books, credit cards, store cards, cash cards and finally debit cards like SWITCH and we have adapted to this change extremely well.

If we can see advantage to our own lives and we can see that the change is well planned, then we welcome change. We need to look for benefits for all the people involved in the process, as the "*what's in it for me?*" syndrome is very powerful.

5.4 People Don't Understand the Technology

Probably quite true, but ask yourself why you need to - we all use a telephone as part of everyday life, but how many of us could really explain how one works? We have technical support people who will address this for us, so don't worry about it. Transacting business electronically must be made as simple and efficient as possible - it should ideally be easier to use than a paper-based system.

5.5 Electronic Trading Isn't Secure

A business transaction, whether paper or any other media, is only as secure as the procedure being followed. It is easy to make electronic transactions secure and auditable, we just need to take this into account. After all, if we submit a paper order to the postal system, how can we be sure it will arrive at the destination? The reality is that our current **processes** are insecure and security is being used as a scapegoat for ET. The answer is that we could opt for a proof of delivery postal service (e.g. an acknowledgement or recorded delivery) and this is exactly what we could do electronically.

5.6 ET is too Costly for the Small Company

Like any new concept, tools for enabling electronic trading were not cheap in the initial years, but as with many new things, they become cheaper with time. As I mentioned earlier, when the radio first came on the market, the cost of a receiver was the equivalent of 8 times the average weekly wage and now we view radios as disposable commodity product. The computer, similarly, is becoming a commodity product and affordable to even the smallest company.

Business cases for the smaller companies can be more difficult to define, as benefits such as:-

- B&Q now save some £1 million every year on telephone calls alone by using ET.
- Peugot-Talbot quote a saving of £16.00 per transaction through paying their suppliers electronically.

are only evident when transaction volumes are high.

However, business cases for ET rarely take into account the other benefits detailed in Chapter 2 and very often the only justification is on a transaction cost basis. This approach is doomed to failure in most instances and will only be successful where the volume of transactions is sufficiently high to warrant justification on these very tactical grounds. This is especially true for the SMEs (Small and Medium Enterprises) and attempts to quantify the more intangible benefits (like inventory and obsolescence savings) must be made.

Businesses should be looking at the more strategic benefits and then the cost of doing ET will become easier to justify. Simply measuring payback is a very short-sighted view of the viability of projects, so please don't fall into this trap. Lack of ET capability is becoming a competitive disadvantage in a number of cases, as more and more companies are looking to persuade their trading partners to do business electronically.

5.7 Why Should We Change?

"The process has worked OK for the last ten years, why should we change it now?" This comment is all too often heard when we look at changing business processes, but in these days of tremendous change in the business world, we can't afford NOT to change.

Charles Handy cited a wonderful analogy in his book "The Age of Unreason" - the Boiled Frog. He maintains that if you place a frog in a pan of water and then slowly bring the water to boiling point, the frog would be boiled alive. The reason? Simply that the frog does not detect the change going on in its surroundings. We can't allow ourselves to become the boiled frogs of tomorrow.

5.8 We Don't Know Where to Start

There are now a large number of organisations around who can provide advice and guidance on starting ET initiatives, from national and international organisations, industry groups, consultancies, specialist information brokers and of course the experienced users (who may be your trading partners). I have included a list of useful addresses at the end of the book that contains a large number of organisations who are prepared to help you.

There are national and international conferences and events (e.g. EDI, ELEDIS and COMPAT) and numerous books, magazines and journals (e.g. the "Electronic Trader" and, dare I hope, this book).

5.9 Summary

This is just a sample of the reasons, excuses and arguments against the adoption of ET in any organisation. There are probably many more "blockers" than these, but the important thing to recognise is the difference between **perceived** blockers and **real** issues. Some people will give you a thousand and one reasons why you shouldn't change something but there are rarely many real issues in doing it.

We need to be able to demonstrate the benefits of ET then the doubters can see what's in it for them. A key to this is measurement - you will need to be able to prove the benefits accrued, so measure the process BEFORE and AFTER ET implementations and just watch the benefits come in - albeit it slowly at first. You can't manage or control a process if it isn't being measured.

View the blockers as the challenge, the hurdles to jump, but don't see them as brick walls.

Plan for the blockers and they won't be a problem.
Don't let the blockers become stoppers.

Part 3

"Understanding the real issues and how to overcome them."

Having now looked at what Electronic Trading (ET) involves, what benefits we should expect from it and some of the perceived implementation blockers, we can now concentrate on examining the real issues in detail and hence prepare ourselves for planning how to overcome them.

An ET programme should not be embarked upon lightly, as it's probably one of the most challenging business issues most organisations will face. After all, companies have been using paper as the basis of their trading for thousands of years and many of our commercial processes date back to the Industrial Revolution of the late 18th and early 19th centuries.

However, with the right level of planning, you should be able to undertake a series of activities that will bring enormous improvements to your organisation - with the wrong level, you could bring chaos!

This section will hopefully provide some of the help you should need to address the cultural, commercial, technical and management issues that may arise, to ensure a well planned and organised implementation. You do need to keep in mind the blockers that I described earlier.

6 People and culture

Before we start considering the human and cultural issues of doing business electronically, let's agree who the players are.

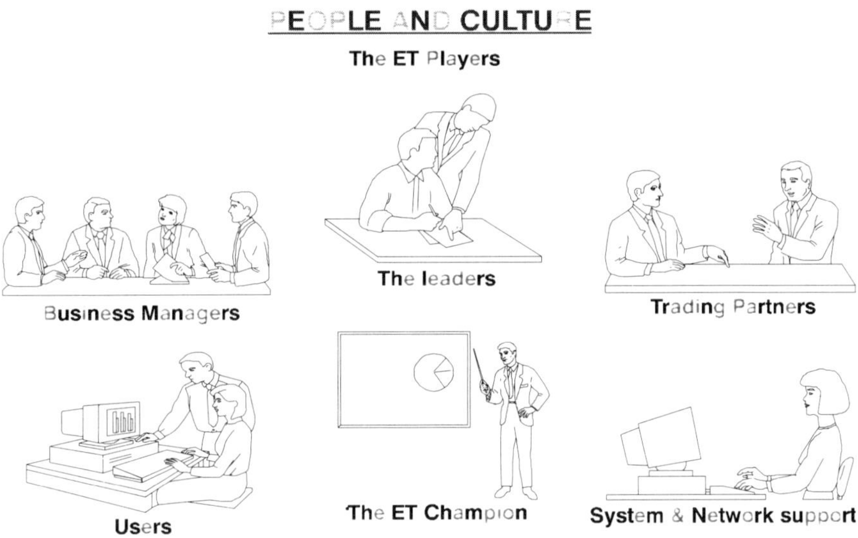

Figure 6-1

Figure 6-1 indicates the different people involved in ET within your own and your trading partners' companies. To successfully implement an ET programme, you must first have the backing and commitment of the most senior managers and board members in the company. Once this has been secured, line managers and business people in general must be on your side and ready to spot the opportunities for exploiting ET techniques. The last group of people that must be willing and able to adapt to ET techniques are the people who provide your systems, whether your own in-house IT department, or an external supplier. Finally, you must also consider your trading partners - it is no use educating and getting the backing of your own company if your trading partners are ignorant of or unwilling to discuss ET. Don't forget that this list of the ET players is replicated in your trading partners' organisations.

6.1 The Approach to ET

ET must be approached in a similar way to Total Quality Management (TQM), the methodology of 'get it right, on time, first time and every time' brought about by a programme of continuous improvement in business processes. Hence, ET needs to become the ordinary day-to-day culture of the organisation before you can say "we are an electronic trading company". So what are the organisational issues that are likely to stop this happening?

Commitment

Firstly, ET must have Board-level commitment - this is not to say that the board must initiate it, but if not, then they must be behind it every inch of the way. It won't be sufficient for the members of the board to say "We must start ET", they must believe it, understand it and make sure that it happens. If they don't really believe it and organise strategy around it, it will be very difficult for the rest of the organisation to become motivated to implement it. There is an aversion to using IT in our businesses that is proportional to the organisational level of the individual in the company, I make this plea to all the senior managers reading these words - lead by example and experience for yourself how easy it is to conduct YOUR business electronically. You can't expect others to follow if you don't provide this leadership.

The Age factor

At a recent ET conference, Sir John Harvey-Jones MBE also attributed this lack of awareness to the age of the people running our companies and certainly our younger employees have been brought up in an IT world and thus find using IT as natural as using the telephone. However, he also concluded that he, whilst always being keen on IT, has used it infinitely more since he retired than he ever did when working. This indicates that the root cause of the problem is the lack of time the managers have to gain an appreciation of what IT can do for them, not necessarily a natural aversion to the technology.

6.2 A Champion for the Cause

Each major part of the organisation (and this may be just one for smaller companies) should have an ET Champion - someone who is an enthusiast and has the persuasiveness to drive ET activities through their part of the company. A lot has been said and written about the seniority and position in the business of the ET Champion. The preferred nominee is a reasonably senior person with very senior backing, but the most important qualification is the fervent belief that he or she can make it work and the credibility of that person in the eyes of the rest of the organisation - whether they are senior, junior, a business person or a technologist. The technology and standards exist, but you do need an ET champion who has the vision, enthusiasm and commitment to make it happen.

6.3 Education for All

I would advocate that one of the major parts of an ET programme (at least in its early days) is education, awareness and promotion. You have to sell a programme like ET from the top to the bottom of the organisation, telling people why they need it, what benefits they are going to get and publicising all their successes.

You are after all changing the culture of the company from paper to electronic trading and people need to understand what's in it for them before they will entertain change. Don't try and force this, because reluctant users are never as successful as converts.

Also, when educating people in ET, don't forget that you may have to include your potential ET trading partners in this. If you are in the envious position of being an ET driver (a "Hub") rather than being driven into it (a "Spoke") by one of your customers, you need to persuade your trading partners as well as internal users. The "virtual company" is a fashionable term to describe the organisation of flexible autonomous business divisions, but this type of company is not going to survive if it can't achieve close integration with its customers' and suppliers' business systems.

Furthermore, consider the messages that your education and training is going to deliver - the Managing Director doesn't necessarily want to hear the same things that a line manager needs to know - you want different training for different groups (managers, end-users, system developers, trading partners). Also, your trading partners may need to be approached in different ways depending on whether they are small, medium or large companies and what value your business means to them.

One way of changing the culture is obviously to get people using some form of ET and as I mentioned in Chapter 1, a simple way of doing this is to install an internal E-mail system. However, this is only feasible if you can justify the cost of doing it and have the luxury of a time-lag before your customers and suppliers are knocking on your door to talk to you about ET. It was marvellous to note that the guide for the 1993 Sunday Times Business Computing show was made available on disc - and advertising space was provided for the more forward thinking companies.

ET, and IT more generally, is changing our organisational structures (the advent of teleworkers demonstrates this) and if we don't address the cultural aspects of these changes then we'll struggle to exploit the benefits they can bring.

A culture is something that you grow - you can't impose it or legislate for it!

7 Commercial Considerations

AT Kearney, a leading UK consultancy, identified in 1990 that EDI was an application that successful companies are more likely to introduce than unsuccessful ones. This is a very strong message to support the need for EDI and for all companies to "think electronic" when considering how to do business. SPAR for example, with its 20,000 grocery stores world-wide has consciously used ET to maintain growth ahead of its rivals and raise the group's profile in the retail world.

In chapter 3 we looked at how electronic trading underpins the Management In The Nineties findings and numerous publications written to examine the commercial problems in our current, turbulent, economic climate have also underwritten electronic business as the way forward. Charles Handy in "The age of unreason" discusses the way information technology has changed and continues to change our commercial world. He postulates on the need for upside-down thinking to address the discontinuity or continuous change in business and ends by hoping that the age of unreason will become the age of greatness.

With all these clear messages coming from such eminent minds, it is hard to argue that business is not going to change. Doing business electronically, as we saw in chapter 4, has been evolving for some time and if, like the ostrich, we bury our heads in the sand, we may ultimately raise our heads to find a world we don't recognise and, more seriously, one that we can't cope with.

Traditionally, large companies have driven ET, thereby reducing the number of trading partners and enjoying a much more strategic relationship with the chosen few. The "hubs" or driving forces behind ET have to date been the customers encouraging their suppliers (the "spokes") to adopt ET techniques such as

EDI, but there are some notable exceptions where this has happened the other way round and indeed Levi are a good example where the drive came from the supply company. No matter which side is the hub, if trading partners are unwilling to join in, they may be viewed as non-strategic thinkers who are not committed to a close partnership and hence may soon find themselves locked out of the trading cycle.

Commitment to ET therefore may help to secure, although not guarantee, a company's future survival. A number of businesses are now insisting on ET as one of their conditions of trade and this is clearly evident in the Retail industry that was at the forefront of the use of EDI.

From the benefits section in Chapter 2, it's obvious that there's a great deal to gain from ET. So let's summarise:-

- the business gurus are saying it's the right thing to do.
- larger companies are now favouring trading partners who can trade electronically.
- there are clear benefits to be gained from ET.

However, having said all this, ET must still be a viable commercial programme for it to be successful in your company and hence there are a number of considerations to be addressed.

7.1 Spotting the opportunities

Firstly, identify where in the business process you are going to start. This won't be an issue if you're being driven into ET because the process will probably be chosen for you, but let's assume for this part that you are the driver. One important aspect of this choice is that you must understand your business processes. That may entail you doing some work in defining these before you select your start point. The process selected for "dipping your toe" in the ET water is one where:-

- it's commercially advantageous for you to do it. For

example, the process is currently inefficient, costly or simply could be improved.

- there are defined (preferably international) standards applicable to the objects to be traded. For example X.400 for E-mail or EDIFACT for EDI.
- you have some persuasive powers over your potential trading partners. For example the purchasing process.

I'm not going to make a great point of competitive advantage here, as I believe that ET is more a case of competitive disadvantage if you don't consider it and with the business turbulence we discussed earlier, today's advantage rapidly turns into tomorrow's necessity. However, there are numerous examples of company's that gain good short term advantage from the application of ET techniques as I will try and cite throughout the book, and Compuserve's recent announcement to issue some of its information on CD-ROM incorporating additional multimedia elements is just one example of this.

Selling the Idea

But let me not digress further. Having selected the process, you then need to sell the concept to the people involved in the process (process operators, users, system suppliers and trading partners). You must plan and execute your persuasion campaign carefully and don't expect it to happen overnight. At the end of it, all must agree that:-

- ET is viable and will improve the process - i.e. they must clearly see the "what's in it for me".
- they have the resources to make it happen.
- they are willing to do it in the same time frame that you require.

You may also have to consider different techniques for different types of trading partners. For example both my own company (ICL) and Texas Instruments needed to find alternatives to EDI for the smaller suppliers we deal with, due to the current, high, entry level costs of EDI. Texas developed an EDI to Fax technique, whilst ICL use the Royal Mail EDIPOST service - in both cases the larger company uses EDI whilst the smaller company receives paper. Not full ET, but a solution to a problem that would probably never have resulted in a totally electronic process.

OK, so you've chosen a suitable process, everyone is persuaded that ET is the right thing to do, so what's stopping you? You need to prepare a business case for doing it (and your trading partner will need to do the same) and get it approved. This will entail you defining the costs involved and the benefits to be gained from adopting ET - from all areas involved.

Interchange Agreements

You then need to consider trading agreements with your partner if you are trading commercial documents, as they will be different electronically from those using paper - for example, how many paper orders have terms and conditions printed on them? In addition to defining commercial arrangements, you may also need to put an interchange agreement in place defining the physical attributes of ET - for example, frequency and times of transmissions, contingency plans if networks are inoperable etc. Organisations like EDIA and CEC have produced standard proforma Interchange Agreements that you should be able to adopt in your own company - there's no point in reinventing the wheel.

The Integrity of Information

Finally, one more thing you need to consider for commercial documents and that is the integrity of the information you currently trade. You would be amazed how much interpretation happens on printed documents ("Oh I know he put that part number, but this is the one that he needs"). Computers can only follow simple instructions, so data integrity is vital when trading electronically. You must be confident that your trading partners can understand all the information you send (part numbers, prices, delivery details etc. etc.).

Opportunities

Opportunities can also arise from the ability that ET can give you, that were simply not possible with previous paper-based processes. Consider the well-publicised case of the US tax preparers, a service industry to the American tax payers. When the Internal Revenue Service (IRS) promoted electronic filing of tax returns, the tax preparers spotted the opportunity to cash in on this concept and started negotiations with financial institutions to collaborate on a system of sending tax payer's information on financial services - only possible because of the information being collected electronically on the tax returns.

Another example of this is American Airlines' seat reservation system (SABRE), again well publicised, but still worth a mention here. When the division responsible for SABRE saw the potential of their system, they began offering booking facilities for ancillary services such as hotels, car hire, etc and their division is now the most profitable part of the company. OTIS Elevators similarly exploited their service management system OTISLINE to offer service capability for other manufacturers' elevator products.

7.2 Legal & Security considerations

With most forms of ET, legality of transactions is not a problem, the issue being more one of security of information. The process where paper documents are being replaced by electronic ones must have its integrity preserved (or enhanced?) and this is no different to ensuring that paper documents are "safe". If you are using a value added network (VAN) to transact electronic documents, the VAN service will provide a number of the measures necessary to ensure this:-

- password control on VAN access.

- audit trails of ET transactions.
- periodic audits of the entire service by a recognised independent 3rd party auditor.

The only thing you should need be concerned with is the archiving of transactions you have sent or received. This however is no different to good standard practice with any computer system.

For sensitive information or transactions where you have a legal obligation on security, you obviously need to review the security and legal aspects in more detail. If the issue is one of non-disclosure of sensitive data, then data encryption will have to be considered. There has been a great deal of work done in recent years on public key encryption systems, so it's not something new. Legality of electronic documents again is an area where a number of organisations have done a great deal of work and the issue today tends to be one of admissibility of evidence rather than one of document legality.

Standards

The X.400 standards for transmission of E-mail and EDI contain various facilities for security, such as non-repudiation, delivery acknowledgement etc. ISO 9796 provides a standard for digital signatures (DIS) and CCITT have developed X.509 that gives recommendations for standard user authentication procedures. Other solutions such as Credit Lyonnais' use of smart cards for electronic signature authentication, are based on a "seal" (condensed file image) to detect alteration in transit.

The main thing is to check what your obligations are in all documents to be traded electronically and then make sure your systems cope with these needs. Again, don't let it become an excuse for not doing it - it isn't a blocker. IT has the potential to greatly enhance the security of your processes, but like a number of other system qualities, security has to be specified as a requirement and designed into the system - you can't easily "bolt it on" afterwards. IT can be used equally successfully to combat fraud as it can to enable it; take Active Analysis' Netmap database tool, which can take information from disparate databases and analyse it to detect organisational relationships being used to carry out fraudulent activities.

7.3 Changing the business process

The last area I would like to consider in the commercial section is changing the business processes - this is where you gain real benefit from ET. Don't be tempted to simply replicate a paper process by an electronic one.

Firstly, go back to basics and ask why do you need the process at all. Once the real reasons and objectives of the process have been established, design an electronic process to achieve these objectives. The process was undoubtedly based on one designed during the Industrial Revolution of the late 18th and early 19th centuries, with the limitations of paper documents in mind and will probably be as appropriate to today's high-tech world as Stephenson's Rocket is to today's railway services. So, it's only sensible to look at the process and examine where it needs changing to reflect modern practices and also, where it can be IMPROVED by adopting ET. However, let me re-emphasise that you cannot start to change business processes that are not fully understood - make sure you have modelled and analysed the process BEFORE you start to change it.

Numerous books have been published which concentrate totally on this subject and I will not pretend to cover the whole subject in depth here, but I would like to take you through a very simple example of changing the business process. Let's consider the ordering cycle process and see how this can be changed to exploit ET techniques. Figure 7.3-1 to 7.3-5 illustrate the changes in the process when moving from paper-based to EDI.

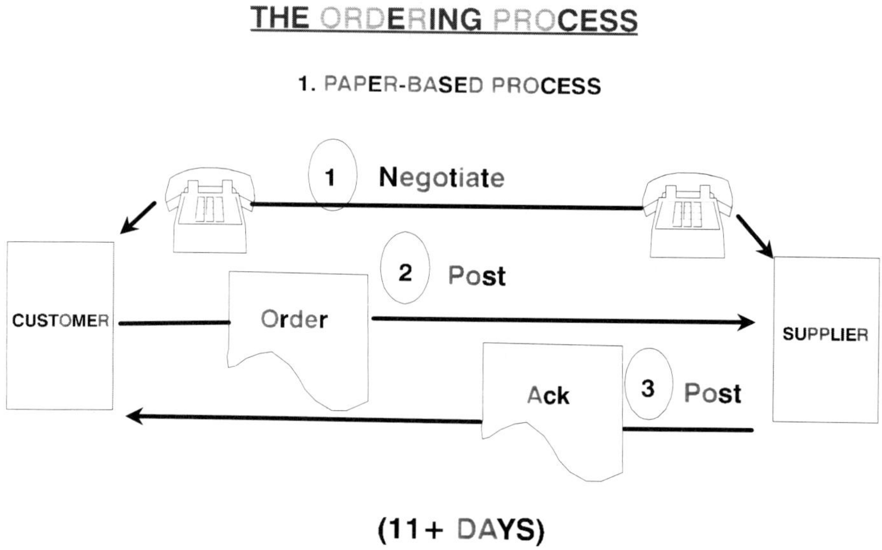

Figure 7.3-1

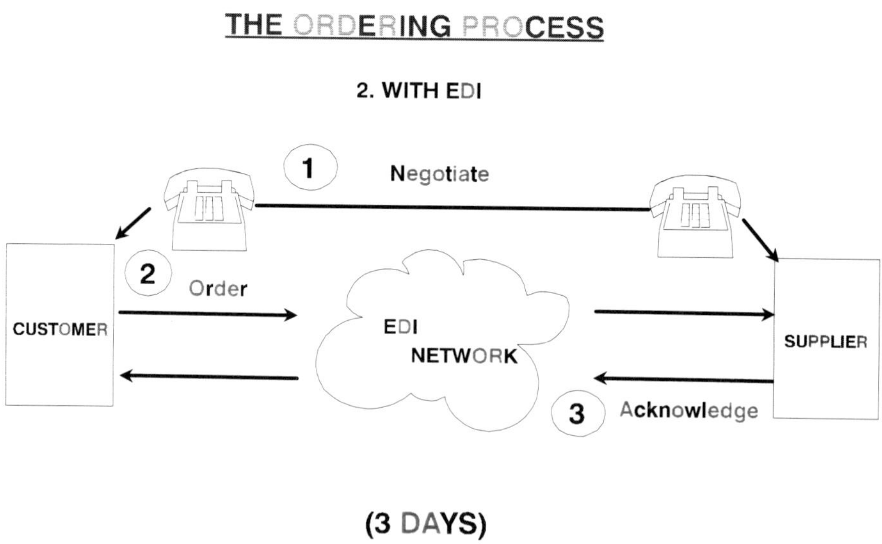

Figure 7.3-2

THE ORDERING PROCESS

3. CHANGING THE PROCESS

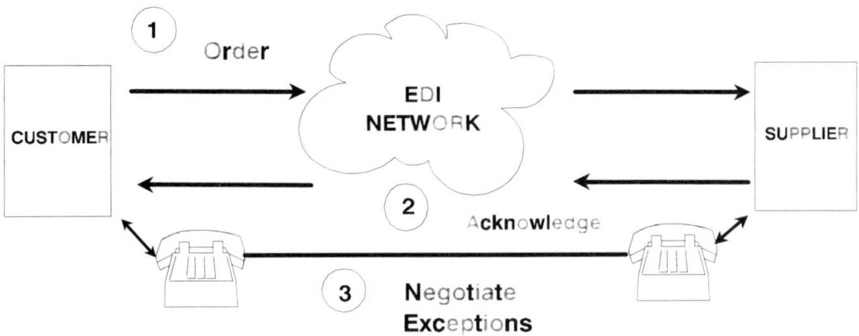

(2- DAYS)

Figure 7.3-3

THE ORDER TO PAYMENT PROCESS

Some of the trade documents that can be sent using EDI

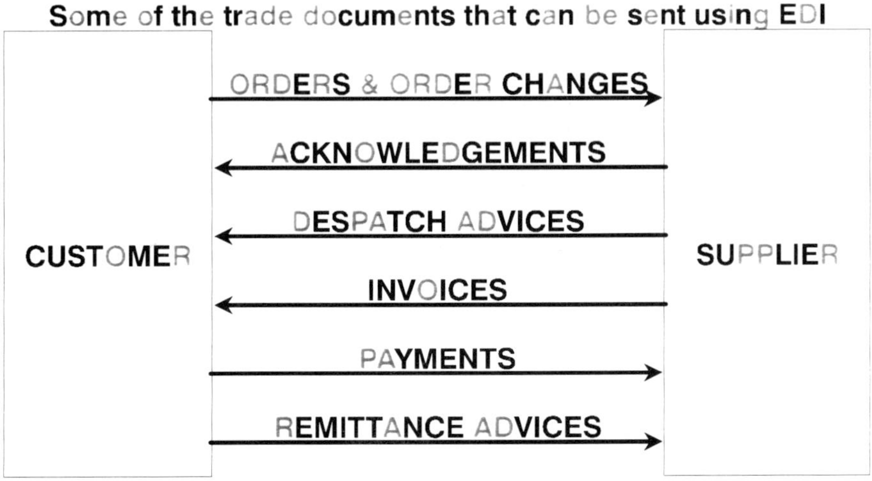

Figure 7.3-4

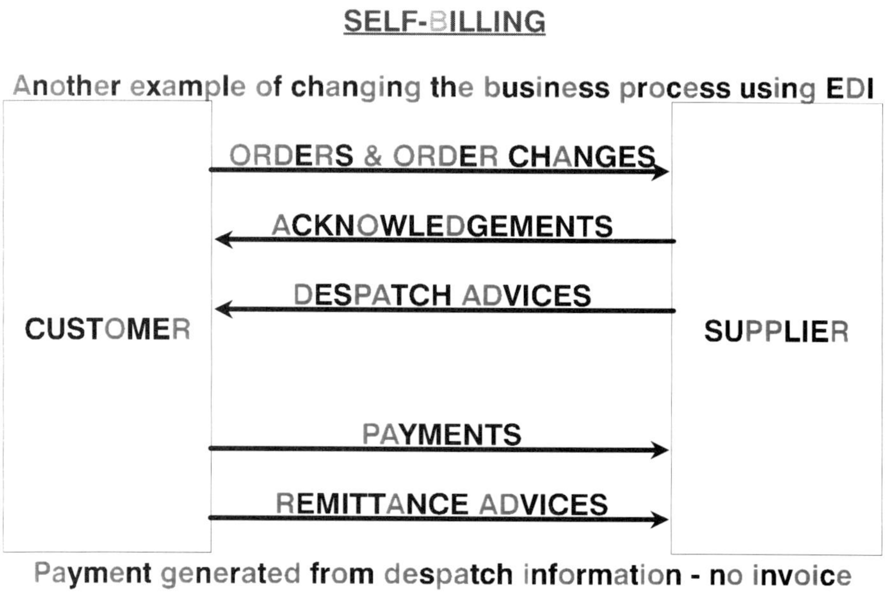

Figure 7.3-5

I don't want to dwell on this topic any further, but this is real business process redesign, reengineering (call it what you will) in practice. Too much has been written on this subject during the past few years for me to add much more and the topic has been subject to much publicity in its alter egos of:-

- Just In Time
- Quick Response
- Total Quality Management
- Business Process Redesign
- Business Process Reengineering

The only difference in all these is the degree of change, but I'll undoubtedly be criticised for even mentioning them all in the same section. Techniques like ET give you the potential to improve your business processes - the degree of change is up to you and your organisation. Some companies can accommodate the large step-function changes whilst others can only cope with smaller incremental change.

One of the best recorded cases of exploiting IT to change business processes is the Batterymarch financial management group in the USA. By using IT to redesign the way it did business, they were able to provide lower priced services to their customers with only a quarter of the staff that their competitors employed. This lead to increased market share, enhanced profitability and early competitive advantage.

Look at how your commercial processes can exploit ET - don't just use it!

8 Standards and networks

I'll split this chapter into two parts, the first section will discuss standards applicable to the objects to be traded and the second section will cover the technology needed to transport these objects - i.e. the infrastructure or network. The subject of developing and enhancing systems to trade electronically will be covered in Chapter 9. The importance of standards and networks in ET implementations is hopefully self-evident, but benefits can be clearly seen when you consider the number of publications and advertisements that now solicit response via E-Mail rather than "snail mail" (traditional surface mail). This is only possible because of standards for addressing, and the interworking network services to transport the E-Mails (via Internet or X.400).

8.1 Standards

The first word of warning here is don't worry too much about standards and technology, and don't let them become an excuse for not doing it, they are not the fundamental issue. Yes, there are areas, for example graphics, where unique international standards have not yet been agreed, but there are plenty of others (e.g. EDI) where standards and technology are not a problem.

You obviously need to understand, or get someone to understand on your behalf, what standard's limitations there are and which are the best areas of ET for you to address first, but there are plenty of organisation around to provide guidance on this:-

- Commerce groups such as Institute of Purchasing and Supply.
- Standards authorities like BSI, ANSI, ISO.
- ET user groups for example, EDIA, EEMA and IDEA.
- Government and other agencies - ANA, EIA, CCITT etc.

- Industry ET user groups such as EDIFICE, CEFIC and ODETTE.
- Specialist "knowledge brokers" such as Cambridge Market Intelligence.
- Your trading partners - especially if they are pushing you!

- you only have to ask!

My word of warning is the adage that "like all good standards there are more than one of them" and this is the real problem - we have proprietary, closed user group, national and international standards and sometimes multiples even in these categories. However, the simple rule is to choose the internationally agreed standard, where one exists.

Private (or proprietary) standards are adequate for internal communications, closed user group ones suffice within one trade sector, national standards will allow communications within your own company and with any other company or trade sector in the same country, but international ones will enable you to trade with everyone in your company, trade sector, country or the world. Furthermore, national standards are now being phased out in many cases in favour of international ones. For example ANSI has announced that they will stop development of their X.12 EDI standards in 1997 in favour of the International EDIFACT standard.

Taking the postal service analogy, if we write in a regional dialect then only people in your locality will be able to read the letter. If we write in the standard language of the country, then anyone in the country would be able to read it. However, if we want people in other countries to be able to read it, then it must be written in a standard internationally recognisable language. Esperanto was intended to be such a language but there was no commercial pressure to drive its introduction and acceptance, and hence English has now been adopted as the European Community's official language.

Varying Standards

One word of warning though, don't assume that because two parties are communicating using the same standard they will necessarily be able to understand each other. For example, I can output a file from my graphics package in CGM (Computer Graphics Metafile) format and read it into my office system using a CGM filter, but the resultant file is gibberish. Why? The answer is interpretation of the standard and in this case the CGM standard has been interpreted in two different ways by the suppliers of the graphics package and the office system. Both you and your trading partner need to agree on the standard AND its interpretation to avoid misunderstandings.

Commercial documents are now almost totally covered by the work that has been done on Electronic Data Interchange (EDI) standards over the past ten years. These standards allow us to exchange structured data between business systems without the need for manual intervention, so a customer's purchasing system can transmit an order to their supplier's sales order processing system, which can respond with an order acknowledgement, despatch advice and then invoice and finally the customer can generate a payment and remittance advice. All this is possible without anyone handling the traded "documents".

Electronic mail systems can "talk" to each other if they both conform to the X.400 standard, but there may be limitations in what can be transmitted, caused by the functionality of the particular E-mail systems. For example, simple text mail messages can be transmitted, but spreadsheets, calendars etc. cannot as there are no agreed standards for these objects.

We now get into the real grey areas, where the standards are prolific at best or non-existent at worst. To exchange graphics, image, software etc. you will have to agree a standard with your trading partner(s), but as this implies, you may find that different partners want different standards and the only real solution will come when international standards are agreed for these objects.

Take for example the CD-ROM, this is a technology that can store the entire Encyclopaedia Brittanica on one disc, but we haven't yet got a commonly agreed standard for the format of these discs.

CALS

The one bit of light at the end of the tunnel in this area is the US Department of Defense's CALS programme, which as mentioned in Chapter 4, looks set to lay down standards for text, image and graphics that will ultimately become international ones. For example:-

- Standard Generalised Markup Language (SGML) for text.
- Group IV Facsimile for raster graphics.
- Computer Graphics Metafile (CGM) and Initial Graphics Exchange Specification (IGES) for vector graphics.
- X.500 for messaging directories.

Later in the book, I'll try to provide some guidance for the system developers to ensure that the standard's issues are confinable and if you find yourself in the position of changing from one to another, this should be possible without any major upheaval.

8.2 Networks

Assuming you've sorted out the standard's challenges, you need to move towards an "Open Systems" environment, where you are not constrained by having to select specific hardware or software to trade with your partners. X.400 and Value Added Networks (VANs) are examples of open system networks, whereas fixed point-to-point links are an example of a closed network solution. Let's look in more detail at what is required to create the open electronic business network for the future.

To address the full trading cycle as we discussed earlier, we may need to transmit Electronic Mail, text, image, 2D & 3D drawings and software in addition to standard trading documents. This requirement to move various types of media together with the fact that a number of our trading partners may be international, leads to some interesting challenges.

Let's look at our requirements for the ideal network. Figure 8.2-1 depicts my, some may say simplistic, view of what the ideal network should look like.

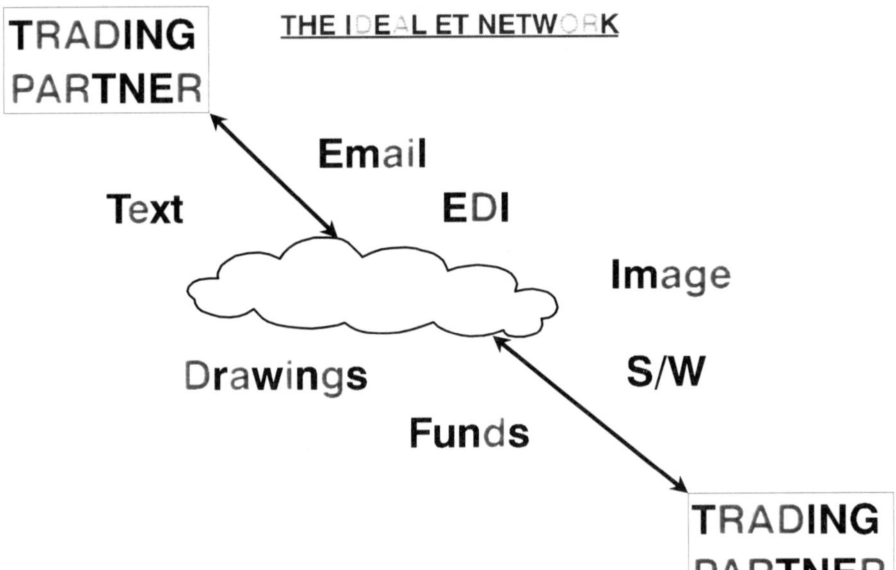

Figure 8.2-1

The requirements are not complicated, they are simply:-

- A one-stop-shop - a single (virtual?) network that is easy to use and will carry any media, anywhere in the world, cheaper, faster and more securely than surface mail operators can provide.
- Technology transparent - The communications service provider to make the link between trading partners transparent of any network technology. We just want a "pipe" that will transport media between us.

For the critics amongst you who will accuse me of being too naive in this statement of requirements, I draw your attention to a presentation at a Telecommunications conference in London by the current Director General of the UK Institute of Directors. He discussed the convergence of computing, communications and information and emphasised that the information content could be expressed in any information media, voice data, text, image, graphics or video. The most remarkable thing about the Director General's point is that it was made in 1985 and yet here we are in the 1990s without much progress to show for it.

Just consider the ideal network against the real world. Our current situation, is far-removed from the requirements for this ideal network and figure 8.2-2 depicts today's typical virtual network - well it **virtually is** a network!

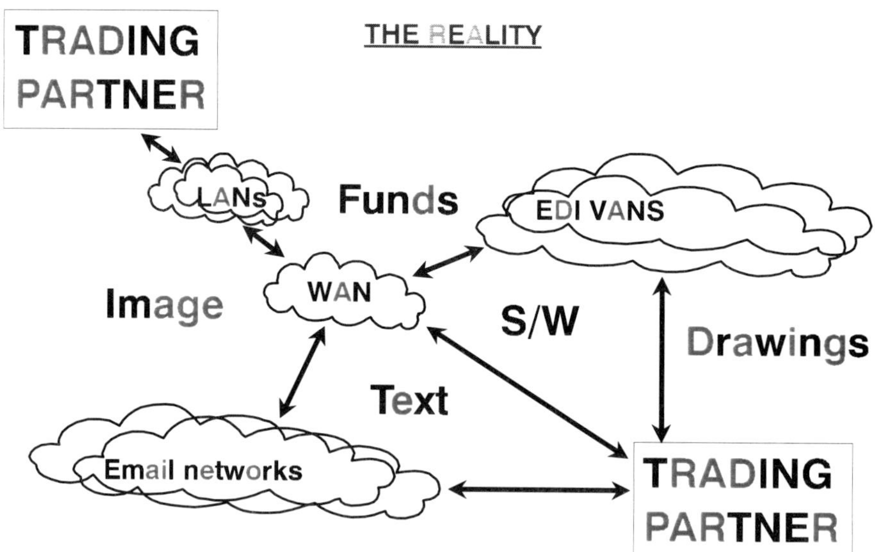

Figure 8.2-2

Network Types

We currently need to use different types of networks:-

- Local Area Networks.
- our internal Wide Area Network.
- multiple Electronic Mail networks.
- multiple Value Added Networks for EDI.

Additionally, we don't have a satisfactory solution for the transmission of certain objects - for example, image, text, funds, software and drawings, due to either lack of standards, multiplicity of standards or network limitations.

8.3 The Issues

The issues that need addressing are:-

Different communications for different media

Because of current network restrictions and limitations, we need to select different networks or communication methods for specific types of media. This choice can be dependent on cost as much as network capability, but still results in multiple communication channels. The ideal system will never become reality until network operators accept that trading between companies involves a number of diverse technologies, not just simple EDI. We need networks capable of accepting trading objects that consist of commercial documents (text and or image), interpersonal messages, software, financial transactions etc. etc.

Incompatibility of network systems

Some of your trading partners may be overseas and or use networks other than the ones used by your company. However, I am constantly being hit with problems such as: "we cannot communicate with company XYZ because their EDI network will not link to our EDI network" or "the electronic mail item was corrupted because their E-mail service is incompatible with ours". These issues are for the network providers to address, we need interworking, compatible networks to successfully trade electronically. I applaud initiatives such as the Asynchronous Protocol Standard (APS) Alliance, but we need more of them. The current arguments concerning interconnection standards between the major EDI VAN companies, for example, must be resolved if we (the customers) are to be provided with the service we need. Regulations in different countries around the world in the past has inhibited much progress in this area, but with the speed of deregulation in the 1990s, this is becoming less valid as an argument by the network providers.

Lack of standards for some media

Great strides have been made in the field of EDI standards over the last ten years, but unfortunately this progress has not been replicated in other areas. E-mail seems to be OK as long as X.400 conformance is possible, but drawings, software, and even simple text are still a problem when selecting standards for transmission. The whole industry must do more to ratify international standards for the transmission of these media.

Service costs

Earlier I said that service cost was as likely to dictate communication method as network capability and this is clearly evident when we look at X.400. A number of the issues detailed could be addressed by trading over X.400, but we can't afford it! The cost of this service is currently prohibitive for use in a number of areas, which is disappointing when we look at the potential of X.400 and X.500. Let me just remind you of part of my requirements for the ideal ET network: "*..will carry any media, anywhere in the world,* ***cheaper***, *faster and more securely than surface mail operators..*" and to this I would just like to add one rider: "*The cost of transport to be as easy to identify as the postal or telephone service*". If network service providers gave us this we would all be happier people.

Addressing

We've a great deal of work to do before we have an international standard for addressing that is unambiguous, and available. The more communications channels we use, the more addresses we need. We have address codes allocated by Article Numbering Associations around the world, network service operators - in addition to X.400 "standard" addressing. Rationalisation is imperative before this situation gets further out of hand.

Use of non-ratified standards over networks

I've been involved in the definition and agreement of standards over a number of years, but the one issue that has become apparent in this area is the (understandable?) view of product and service providers to non-ratified standards - they are very loath to accept them. However, the standards ratification process is so lengthy that use of non-ratified standards is necessary in order to take early advantage of ET. Whilst I accept a certain amount of reluctance from the product and service providers, I think they must begin to take a more lenient view.

Bandwidth requirements for image and other media

I stated my requirements earlier as a "pipe" between trading partners. If this "pipe" for carrying electronic objects needs to be particular widths for specific types of objects then the network operators should be addressing this need. We don't want different "pipes" for different objects and if this means variable bandwidth networks then so be it. Moreover, we don't want to be asked what width the pipe should be, we want to specify our requirements in business terms, not technological ones. Consider the predictions being made for fibre optics:- capable of handling 40 million calls simultaneously within a decade (this compares with 2000 in the late 1980s, 9000 in 1993 and 40,000 in 1995) and this is being achieved by simply improving the equipment that connects the cable, not the cabling itself. We can see why we need this increased capability when consider the systems we are using today:- an ASCII format file of 600 words is approximately 4k bytes, but in some of our latest PC word processing systems this can be easily be doubled. We need to capitalise on this bandwidth capability in order to deliver the full potential of ET.

Service provider interpretation of standards

This issue was certainly prevalent in the early use of EDIFACT standards, but does not appear to be a problem currently with the network. The problem however can still arise in the area of EDI translation products, and in the connection of E-mail services to X.400 networks. As we improve our definition of standards, we must strive to remove any ambiguities from them.

End-to-end auditability of multiple-VAN use

My own company has been very diligent in the auditability of ET transactions, but one area that still gives cause for concern is connection to trading partners via multiple networks. The audit we get is to the VAN gateway and not to our trading partner's mailbox. This is not sufficient for our audit requirements, we must be able to provide a complete end-to-end management and audit of our ET transactions.

8.4 Everyday "networks"

I thought it would now be worthwhile drawing a parallel with the approach taken by some of our more common everyday consumer service "networks" in order to identify the type of service we require for ET transmissions.

Telephone operators

To make a telephone call to almost anywhere in the world, I simply pick up my BT phone and dial. I also have a telephone book that identifies the cost of making the call. When I receive my bill, I can see the exact (total) cost of the call, assuming I have opted for itemised bills. This process is simple, relatively quick and the cost is easily identifiable and paid to my prime service provider.

Air travel

I need to fly to some remote part of South America, which means a number of different flights to get to the airport close to my destination. To arrange this I simply contact a travel or ticket agent, give them the start and end destinations and they do the rest. I do not need to worry about how many planes or indeed airlines I will be flying on, and the only bill I pay is to the agent.

Postal service

Letters to the far side of the world are as easy to send as one to mother down the road. They may take a bit longer to get there, but the process is the same as for national post except that the stamp will cost more and you have the choice of surface or air mail.

The reason I have identified these three services is that:

- the processes are easy to use and familiar to all of us.
- in all cases, the prime service contractor provides a complete service, even though they involve multiple service providers.
- the destination address is easily identifiable.
- the cost of the service is readily available.

If we now compare these services with the current state of ET communications methods, we can see that there is a great deal of improvement to be made before our network services come anywhere near our telephone, air and postal services. There appears to be a big void between the end user and network service providers and this chasm must be bridged if we are to have consumer type network services within our businesses. It also demonstrates something that is prevalent in business today and that is the reluctance to insist on the type of service for our companies that we all demand as part of our everyday, personal lifestyle.

TLAs

However, having said all this, I think I've spotted a trend in the networking service industry. Just as its parent, the IT industry, networking has suffered from the Three Letter Abbreviation (TLA) syndrome over the years and we can see this clearly in terms such as: LAN, WAN, VAN, X.25, etc. Networking then obviously felt it was far more complicated than the rest of the IT field and decided it needed FLAs (yes, you've guessed - Four Letter Abbreviations) and hence terms such as FDDI, ISDN, X.400, X.500, etc. came into common use. However, recent press statements lead me to believe that Asynchronous Transfer Mode (ATM) is the answer to all our prayers, at least as far as variable bandwidth is concerned (although I don't pretend to be an expert in networking technology) - but this is a TLA! If this really is a trend in networking to a more simplified terminology (and technology?), then I openly welcome this pattern. Please let us talk about our requirements in business not technological terms.

Gateways and Messaging

Before I finish this chapter, let me just identify two other aspects of networking that need careful thought and planning - corporate gateways and message control. For the smaller companies gateway architecture may not be a problem, but the larger ones will need to consider this architecture for access to external services. There is no right way and wrong way to go about this, but you need to decide how you want your trading partners to see you and take the appropriate steps to ensure that your gateway strategy supports this.

For example:-

- Do you have a single external gateway for all ET, in which case X.400 is probably the answer?
- Will single gateways for different objects such as EDI, E-mail etc. be the right solution?

- Are multiple gateways for different parts of the company needed, in which case your trading partners will see you as different organisations and you obviously have the cost of all these gateways?

The key message here is plan what your external gateway strategy will be - preferably before you start, as changing subsequently could be difficult and expensive.

Also, message control is an equally important aspect for consideration. Different forms of telecommunications offer different levels of message control and it is important to recognise these variations and understand what your network service supplier will provide and what you will need to do to supplement this. For example, when we consider the Value Added Network (VAN) and X.400, the products and services for VANs will undoubtedly offer a higher level of message control than equivalent products and services from X.400 providers. It is important not to overlook this as it can have a major effect on the overall cost of the service and the amount of work you are going to have to do to use it.

Standards and Networks are only a problem because of the variety, not the lack, of choice.

9 Developing your Systems for ET

There are a number of areas to be considered when developing business systems capable of trading electronically:-

- The style of user interaction.
- Alignment of systems to process, roles and modes, not functional applications.
- System architecture, especially component separation.
- Standards for electronic objects.

The following sections attempt to address each of these areas and provide guidance to the system developers for building the electronic systems of the future. However, it should also help users and business analysts start defining their requirements for electronic trading systems, as good system design starts in the requirement specification stage and it's often too late to "bolt on" the facilities retrospectively.

When the UK Training and Enterprise Councils (TECs) started looking at ET, they quickly spotted that the technical problems had largely been solved by the suppliers of electronic links and they needed to focus on how the links would effect the way they do business, the relationship with their trading partners and the common interpretation of the standards they would be using.

This demonstrates that the technology isn't a major problem, it's the processes and interpretation of the standards that need attention.

9.1 The style of user interaction

For some years now, we have been developing systems to take advantage of the technology presented to us. This has resulted latterly in the development of on-line, interactive systems that assume a "warm body" is sat in front of a screen inputting data to the system and reacting to messages and other information sent to the screen by the system.

We have seen input devices evolve from the older style punched and magnetic cards or tape data entry machines, to the now beloved keyboard and mouse. More recently we have seen specialist devices such as scanners, point-of-sale terminals and bar-code readers, and now we are seeing the advent of specialist equipment such as Apple's Newton, a Personal Data Assistant (PDA) capable of turning handwriting into computerised text.

These developments are all aimed at improving the entry of information into our systems, but it's important that we don't assume that all input to the system will be manually entered, no matter how efficiently.

Similarly, the traditional output device for business systems has been the old favourite printer. On-line terminals have aided our transition from paper to electronic information in some small way, but how many times do we see people take a printed copy of their VT screen? The output devices of the future will be very different from today's limited capability. Already you can output a word processing document directly from your PC to an electronic Fax gateway and hence the only paper produced is within the recipient's organisation (unless of course they have a Fax gateway and can deliver the document via E-mail to the user). However, companies such as Ricoh and Rank-Xerox are now developing ranges of office machines that can be controlled from your PC and soon you will be able to access voice (telephone, voice mail, video conferencing) and document (photocopiers with language translation facilities) services from your desk top.

All these improvements in input and output devices will change the way our systems are designed, but ET still demands a further difference in the style of user interaction. ET trading partners cannot be assumed to be within the same organisation, geography or time-zone as other users of the system and hence it is less likely that responses from remote trading partners will be real time.

Therefore, when defining and building user interaction functionality, we should assume that the user is remote from the system and may even be in another organisation in a different company. The "user" may also be another system - for example, if system A wants information from system B, the interaction can generate an enquiry on system B as though the request had emanated from a person not a system.

The concept of object request brokers in client-server systems is an example of this idea. Moreover, client-server systems are necessary to implement a true electronic trading system, with the client (customer) requesting information from the server (supplier), or vice versa.

Delivery

Care needs to be taken when designing system output, so that it can be delivered electronically. For example, the majority of computer reports I see are still designed for 11" 132 character wide continuous stationery, when what we really need are reports that are able to be viewed on line - i.e. with current technology restrictions, 80 column portrait documents ideally with an index for easy access on a screen.

Delivery of output also needs due consideration:-

- Does the user want to process the figures contained in a report? If so, will a spreadsheet be more appropriate than a document?
- Deliver output via electronic mail rather than printing.

To a great extent, this is an area for considering the separation of the output mechanism from the system - more about component separation in section 9.3 - after all, why does it matter to the business system that an object is to be printed, sent via E-mail etc. An example of this in ET is the use of the UK Royal Mail's EDIPOST service - a system can generate EDI transactions and some will be sent directly to the trading partners (obviously those who are capable of processing EDI messages) and others will be sent to the Royal Mail who print the paper document and posts it to the trading partner. Furthermore, the EDIPOST service can now be extended to generate electronic responses from trading partners who received paper documents, by making innovative use of touch tone telephones.

I'm sure you can all think of a number of other examples of how to provide user interaction styles appropriate for electronic trading, but let me end this section with a simple question for you to ask yourself when you're designing future systems:-

- How will the system interact if the "user" is a laptop computer connected to a network?

9.2 Processes not functional applications

The alignment of systems should be to process, roles and modes, not to functional applications. In the 1970s and 1980s, computer (application) systems were designed to support specific functional areas of the business - for example, accounts, purchasing etc.

Although systems designed during the recent years are evolving away from this functional approach, we still do not align our systems to business process. With the current trend of Business Process Redesign or Reengineering, we must become more process oriented in our system design. Systems should be built in modules that support roles in an organisation and then a full business system can be built from a combination of role based modules to support whatever process is defined. This approach also gives us the flexibility to adapt our systems to changes in the business far easier than if they were built to support functional activities.

The concept of Business Process Modelling, Analysis and finally enactment will never be feasible until our systems are designed to support this.Most of the major IT companies are now promoting open systems architectures that have been developed with this concept in mind - for example ICL's **OPEN*framework***.

9.3 System architecture - component separation

One aspect of system architecture that is fundamental to ET is component separation and again you will find that publications such as ICL's **OPEN*framework*** will cover this in greater detail than I am going to do here.

IBM recently stated that with an ET architecture, even for internal processes, the business can make fundamental organisation changes quite readily without the computer systems being a limiting factor.

The systems of the future will hold more than textual information (e.g. image and sound objects) and as we discussed earlier, will have different styles of interaction than traditional functional-based system such as Sales Order Processing, Stock Control etc. They will also run on multiple hardware platforms with, for example, a PC user interface, UNIX processor and mainframe data store.

As ET is an area where open, distributed systems, capable of handling non-textual information, component separation is vital,

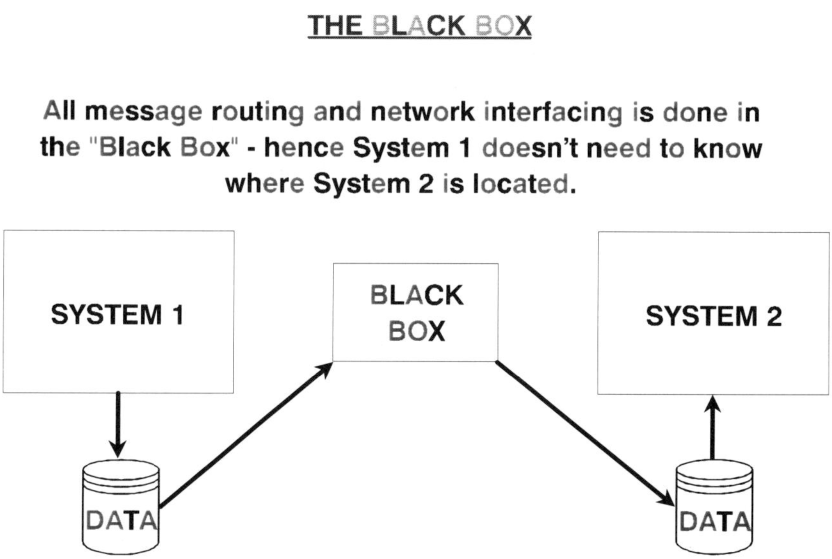

Figure 9.3-1

especially when considering the interfacing and networking layers of a system. Consider Figure 9.3-1, which depicts the need for separation of the networking layer from the business system. If we divorce the message routing and network connection from the system then we obviously make our system more open and maintainable for the future.

Other areas for separation are user interaction and media covered in section 9.1, and also standards. Standards now exist for a large number of trading objects (see Chapter 8), but in order to ensure that our systems are future proof from changes in standards, translation should be undertaken outside the system by a module dedicated to this function. Figure 9.3-2 shows how this separation could be achieved.

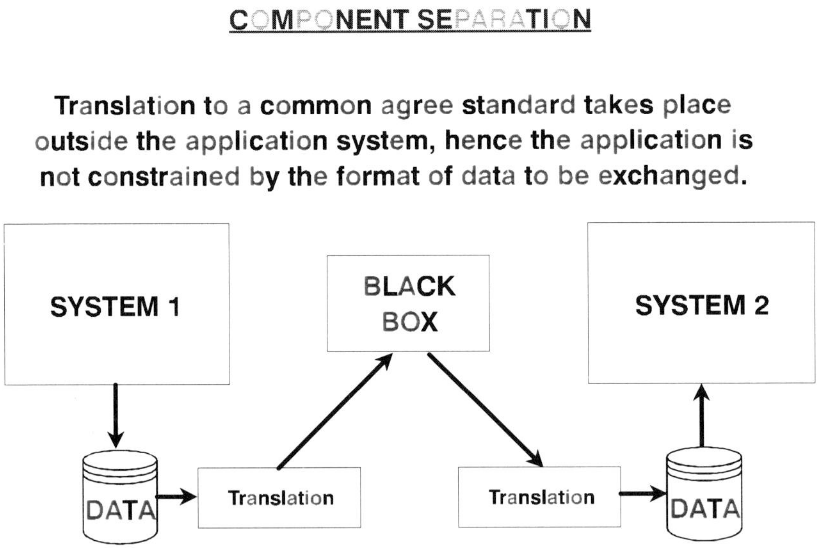

Figure 9.3-2

However, the standards we are going to use do also have an impact on the way systems are to be built for the future - the information stores we design should take into account standards for the objects they want to store and Section 9.4 will expand on this. Consider a Geographical Information System (GIS), this type of system will be vastly different in storage requirements and interaction style than, for example, a general ledger system.

Component Reuse

Component reuse is not something that is needed for ET, but is simply good system practice. However, with the need to build systems quicker and with more flexibility to cope with tomorrow's business, it is a vital part of future systems. I was an avid fan and driver of the Ford Capri and you can imagine my disappointment when this lovely car was withdrawn from the market. Had Ford gone mad, I asked myself? When I confronted a Ford dealer on this, the answer I got proved that Ford had taken the right decision - the Capri was becoming a one-off. Its demise had been caused by the lack of reuse of standard components - the brakes, lights etc. were all Capri-specific and Ford could no longer afford the expense of this non-standard car.

ET Applications

Before ending this Chapter, I would just like to briefly consider one topic - electronic trading applications. By ET applications, I don't mean systems that have been designed or enhanced to enable electronic trade within a specific business process, I mean systems that are designed specifically for ET. This will be covered more in the futures section in Chapters 11 & 12 as most of these systems are yet to be written, but let me just mention one system that exists currently and holds great store for the future - the electronic catalogue. This system is designed to replace traditional paper catalogues and can potentially save major retailers inventory costs by the ability to hold sample stocks on the electronic catalogue rather than in-store. Think also of the potential for property agents holding details of real estate for sale, do-it-yourself stores offering help and advice on carrying out those jobs around the house in addition to the materials needed to do it, etc.

9.4 Standards for electronic objects

As I mentioned in the last section, the standards we are going to use have an impact on the way our systems must be built in the future - the information stores we design in future should take into account standards for the objects they want to store:-

- International EDI standards (EDIFACT) exist which define not only file formats for traded documents, but also data element definitions (ISO 7372) - for example currency codes, units of measure, name and address sizes and many, many more. But how many of us take these into account when defining new databases?
- Application Programming Interfaces (APIs) exist for connecting to X.400 services and accessing X.500 directories.
- Standard Generalised Mark-up Language (SGML) for text.
- Group IV Facsimile for raster graphics.
- Computer Graphics Metafile (CGM) and Initial Graphics Exchange Specification (IGES) for vector graphics.

Chapter 8 contains more details on the standards applicable to ET and also gives sources of information on the standards

9.5 Summary

I hope in this chapter that I have given you some food for thought to start questioning the way we are currently building business systems. The systems of the future will operate quite differently from the ones we are using today, otherwise we'll find it very difficult to remain competitive.

System analysts, designers and developers have key roles to play in the enabling of ET, but this will only happen if they take the trouble to understand what ET is all about and how to create systems that will support this new way of doing business.

System builders must also consider how **they** will trade electronically in the future, in the elements of the system that the users don't necessarily see:-

- system development tools
- transaction management
- system management

ET isn't just about business people exchanging commercial documents, it's also about IT people trading electronically.

The tools we use to build systems must be capable of communicating electronically, but CASE tools have had a rather chequered career to date and open repositories even more so. This has been the result of standards issues and whilst many suppliers originally pinned their hopes on the Information Resource Dictionary System (IRDS) range of standards, this failed because there were two of them; one developed in America by ANSI and one from Europe that became an ISO standard. A separate European standard, the Portable Common Tool Environment (PCTE), was defined but floundered because it was all-embracing and became too cumbersome. The leading contender now appears to be the CASE Data Interchange Format (CDIF), but watch this space.

Transaction management in open, distributed systems needs far more consideration than in proprietary single-platform ones. The key to this is once again standards and Open Transaction Management (OTM) is a key area of work within both ISO and X/Open currently. I do not intend devoting much more space to this topic as it is far more complex than any summaries I could hope to provide here. The reason for this complexity is that a transaction needs to be considered at different levels (i.e. on the ISO 7-layer model) and I would rather recommend the books to be read than provide a simplistic overview than would probably be of little value. Further publications on this and other ET subjects can be found in the bibliography section at the back of the book.

The systems we build should also be capable of trading electronically in the information we need to manage them, and open system management techniques are of paramount importance in the world of open distributed business systems. However, standards are again a problem here and although the OSI management framework (the Common Management Information Protocol [CMIP]) appears to be the most open of these, the Internet management framework (Simple Network Management Protocol [SNMP]) and the Distributed Management Environment (DME) from the OSF can't be ignored.

Include electronic trading in the system development and management process, don't just assume that it effects the application functionality.

10 Managing the Implementation

If I was asked to rank the Chapters of this book in order of importance to successful Electronic Trading (ET), then this would have to be number one. The reason why so little apparent progress has been made on ET, compared to the predictions that continue to be made by the pundits, is simply that it is far more complicated to manage than other programmes and projects, and also more of a culture shock.

However, the pressures to trade electronically are ever increasing; for example, Lloyds of London told its brokers that they must adopt ET by a certain date or the future of the insurance market was in question. Just 10 weeks prior to the deadline only two-thirds of the brokers had signed up and only 15% of business was being done electronically. Why? One key reason was that they had not defined the interface between Lloyds and the broking community - i.e. they didn't understand how they were going to trade using this new method of doing business.

The world recession has emphasised the need to make our commercial processes even more efficient than ever before and yet it can also make the implementation of new systems more difficult. The Swedish project, Neutral Intelligent CAD Communication (NICK), certainly found this when the project was suspended due to financial problems.

ET alone though will not solve the world's business problems unless the systems we use are designed for this method of trade. Miguel Ganose, the Technical Director of British American Consulting Group (BACG), recently highlighted this point when he said that EDI is the **method**, not the solution and stated that it was no good if an order arrived two days before delivery was due when the production systems couldn't cope with this quick turnround. The points made in the last Chapter are of paramount importance if this situation is to be avoided.

Certainly, with an ever turbulent business world, pressure from our trading partners to adopt ET and the need to reengineer our processes and systems to trade this way, managing an ET programme becomes a vital piece of the jigsaw.

I would like to consider this management task under three headings:-

- The people involved in ET.
- Key activities for successful electronic trading.
- Establishing an ET programme.

I will then end this Chapter with a brief look at putting together a business case for ET.

10.1 The people involved in ET

During the years I worked in information systems development, I came to learn that the more departments that were involved in a project, the more difficult it was to manage and implement. The sole reason for this is that all parties have different needs, motivations and pressures, and hence need overall management to ensure that activities are co-ordinated and completed on time.

If we accept this basic philosophy of project management, just think who is involved with an ET project. Figure 10.1-1 shows what is involved in implementing electronic interfaces between two organisations, whether within your own company or with an external partner, and from this we can determine the players in the game:-

- Business users - the people responsible for the definition and maintenance of the process, those who manage the operation of the process and the end users involved in the actual day-to-day operation of the process. So it's not just

ELECTRONIC INTERFACING METHODOLOGY

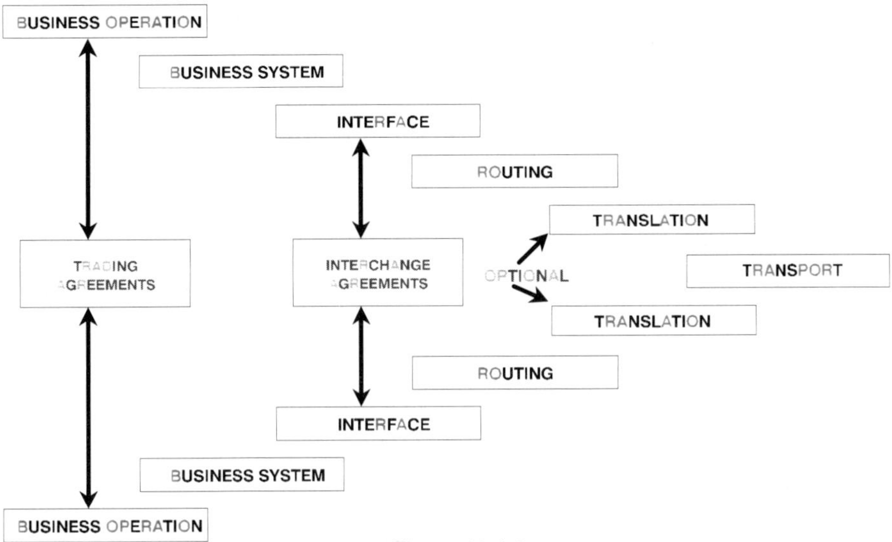

Figure 10.1-1

the process operators, it's also their management and whoever is responsible for the process definition.

- Agencies - the organisations and people responsible for certain controls that may be placed on the information you are trying to trade. For example, legal, treasury and commercial departments, banks, tax authorities, distribution agents (customs, freight handlers etc.) and there are probably many more.
- System developers - the people responsible for maintaining the information system that supports the process and the interfaces necessary to link it to another organisation's system.
- Standards authority - the person or persons who understand what standards exist and what needs to be done to convert to and from the standards.
- Network technicians - those responsible for routing and transporting your electronic messages within your own company and, if necessary, to and from an external network.
- Network operators and service providers - the organisation(s) that support any external network systems you may need.

- Project Manager - the person within your organisation who will take control of the ET project and the activities being undertaken by all the above.

This demonstrates that there are a number of different and diverse organisations and roles involved in ET and don't forget that for links with external partners, this list is replicated within your trading partner's organisation - your project manager will have to work with his or her counterpart in the other company and one of the project managers needs to provide overall project leadership.

You may have to consider some sort of project board, steering group or other method of ensuring that communication between all the interested parties is carried out effectively. British Gas for example use an ET Steering Group to ensure a consistent approach to its trading partners.

10.2 Key activities for successful electronic trading

Let's now consider implementing a simple electronic link between a customer and supplier and the major steps to be taken in this project:-

- Before you can even thinking about the rest of these activities, you must decide who your trading partner will be. This may seem to be a trivial point, but trading partner selection is an art form in itself. Any company needs to be able to put together a business case for ET, so don't assume that just because you have justified it, your partner can also do the same. I remember when one of our purchasing managers tried to put pressure on an international company to accept ET, but he didn't realise that, although the amount of business in question was very large, it was only large in our terms and represented less than 1% of the other company's turnover - you can imagine the response he got.

- Customer and supplier must meet and firstly agree in principle to trade electronically and then select what it is they are going to trade. They may decide to start at the beginning of the trade cycle with interpersonal mail or Quotations or Orders, or at the other end of the cycle with

Invoices and or Payments. However, the main point here is to establish at the outset what the implementation is to achieve and agree the scope and detail of the pilot. This initial meeting may need various members of the project in attendance, as decisions will be taken on the process to be addressed and the trading documents to be exchanged - which may have commercial, standard's, system and network implications.

- After this initial agreement to trade electronically has been reached, it is important to consider whether there are any commercial implications. For example, do customer and supplier agree on what products they trade and how they will identify them (you will find that there can be a great deal of interpretation goes on with a printed purchase order), does your purchasing agreement cover electronic trading (terms and conditions are often printed on the back of a printed order), if Invoicing is involved you may need to involve the tax authorities to get clearance to trade electronically - ET is different to paper trading, so don't overlook this activity.

- The next step will be to examine what changes are required to your information systems. At the very least you will need to be in a position to process a file of electronic transactions - either producing this file from your system or receiving and processing one received from your trading partner.

- You then need to define how the electronic communication will physically take place. What standards conversion do you need? Do you and your trading partner have the same interpretation of the standard being used? Do you need hardware and software to connect to an external network? Will you need more than one external network? Interchange agreements are needed for electronic links between organisations, and bodies such as SITPRO have standard documents that can be used for this. Don't forget though to make sure that both your commercial agreements and interchange agreements are maintained under change control, they are not documents that should be set in concrete.

- Assuming that the project is still feasible, the project managers on both sides now need to work out how much it's going to cost, put the business case together and start to plan the activities in detail.
- Once the project initiation occurs, it is vital to maintain good communications between all parties involved - I've seen tremendous problems caused simply because people didn't know what was going on.

Obviously, project management is a key role in ET and a lot has been said about whether the project manager should be a business user or an IT person. I don't think that this argument will ever reach a final conclusion because the most important qualities of an ET project manager are:- tenacity; good communication, interpersonal and negotiating skills; knowledge of business and IT; and obviously good project management skills. The business person who is IT aware is equally as qualified as the IT person who is business aware to perform this role, so don't get too embroiled in this argument.

10.3 Establishing an ET programme

I mentioned ET programmes and projects at the beginning of this Chapter and so far, I've only talked about projects. I hope by now that you will have seen that ET projects are complicated, but I also hope that following the previous two sections, you can feel confident about taking on one of these projects. My definition of a programme is a collection of projects aimed at achieving different parts of a common objective.

One point I keep emphasising about ET is that it is not just about one particular type of link and we would be wrong therefore to restrict ET to simple EDI, E-mail etc., we must think more holistically. When we trade with another individual, department, organisation or company, we exchange various objects of information as we discussed in the very first Chapter of the book.

I will define an ET programme, therefore, as a collection of ET projects brought about to address different aspects of the trading exchanges. You may have:-

- A document control project to provide an electronic document service in the company.
- An image project to exchange drawing information with designers and manufacturers.
- An EDI project, or more than one if for example you have decided to attempt EDI with both customers and suppliers, or you are applying EDI to different business processes.
- An E-mail project to implement an internal E-mail service, or link your existing service to customers and suppliers.
- A business information project to look at non-EDI business documents in the form of, for example, spreadsheets and business forms.
- The list is endless....

Sitting above all this is someone who has the vision to see what's possible by employing electronic methods and who can keep track of all the ET projects being undertaken. This "ET Champion", like the project manager, should be both business and IT aware (i.e. the "Hybrid" manager phenomenon), but must also be of a high enough level of seniority or persuasiveness to give them the credibility to "make things happen". Enthusiasm is a powerful driving force but it must go hand in glove with credibility.

10.4 The business case for ET

I've lost track of how many papers, articles and conference presentations I've seen addressing the business case for various aspects of ET and a lot of very eminent people have written and said a great deal about this subject. ET is and will always be difficult to cost justify. Certain projects may prove easy - for example when we first implemented EDI links with our suppliers, we calculated that we would save 40% of the cost of producing a paper order and hence cover our development and implementation costs. However, this was probably the exception to the rule and the business case we put forward didn't do justice to the real benefits gained - such as:-

- Reduction in order cycle time from 13 to 2 days.
- Inventory savings.
- Improved productivity from purchasing staff.
- etc., etc.

Nor did it do justice to the real objective behind the EDI project, which was a business aim to reduce our time to market. Remember that the whole range of benefits for ET are reviewed in Chapter 2.

One last point worthy of mention at this juncture is that an ET project driven by the IT department can be difficult to implement, unless it is clearly driven as supporting a business goal. Whatever it is you're trying to do, there must be a business objective that an IT project supports. Once this is established, ET, like any other IT project, should then be justified in terms that indicate how it supports that business objective.

GEC Plessey Telecommunications (GPT), for example, started an EDI project to achieve zero defects, ship-to-stock, 100% on-time delivery, 100% service performance, reduced lead times, optimum utilisation of resources and ultimately, reduced cost of ownership - all good business drivers, but I just hope they put the measurement in place to monitor their performance against these critical success factors. Superdrug estimate that electronic Invoices will reduce processing time from 5 to 2 minutes and at 500 invoices a week, this is quite a saving AND easily measurable. In addition to demonstrating how objectives should be easily measurable, this is also an example of a company with the luxury of sufficient volumes to justify ET on cost saving alone and although Sir John Harvey-Jones stated at a recent ET conference that EDI pays for itself in paperwork savings alone, this tends to be true only for the companies with larger volumes.

There are no right or wrong ways to justify ET and the reasons for doing it are very diverse, however if ET can't be linked to a business objective then there will be difficulty in putting a case together which doesn't simply rely on the old cost-benefit equation. Bench marking your processes against other companies and competitors is also a very useful way of providing evidence for a business case, assuming of course that you can demonstrate a way of making your processes better than the company you are benchmarking yourselves against.

Many of the discussions about ET state that you need "corporate commitment" or "management buy-in" or some equally pretentious phrase, when what they really mean is that you need a good solid business case. Senior managers only listen to proposals that save money or improve the business, so define the case in these terms and link it to an objective that they have visibility of, or forget it - "put up or shut up".

With the business benefits described in Chapter 2, I trust that you'll now be in a position to put together a business case for ET. Note, there isn't a standard formula for this business case, or indeed a generic set of benefits, every implementation of ET will need to be considered on its own merit.

10.5 Summary

I hope that this chapter has helped satisfy the "How to do it" aspects of ET. I don't pretend to have all the answers, none of us do, but I trust that I've added to your understanding of who is involved in ET projects, what the key activities for implementation are, the importance of thinking holistically and strategically about ET, and the need to think carefully about the business case. Suffice it to say at this point that I firmly believe that the Programme and Project Managers will make or break your ET implementation, so pick them carefully.

Also, don't think that if you get everything in this Chapter right you'll automatically have a successful ET programme. I said at the beginning of the Chapter that, in my view, this was the most important part of the book, but I didn't mean to the exclusion of the other sections. The whole book is meant to be a blueprint to successful ET, managing the implementation is just one, albeit very important, element. I see the management aspect as the "glue" to the whole programme, but the other components must be in place for the glue to stick to.

ET programme management is vital for success, so don't make it the responsibility of the "office boy".

Part 4

The future of Electronic Trading

As we've seen, the recent advances in the use of Electronic Trading (ET) has emanated from, and initiated further, improvements in the technologies and standards needed to trade electronically, but what can we expect from the future?

The following pages seek to identify some of the known improvements that we can expect and also hypothesise on some of the more speculative ones. It will suggest new possible scenarios and hopefully provide "food for thought" for you to take away and mull over at your leisure - assuming you have any leisure time between ET activities.

If I'm successful, the following two chapters should be the most controversial of the whole book. I want you to question my thoughts, ideas and proposals, because only when you start questioning do you begin to realise what the future can hold.

Remember that if you do nothing, the only thing that's certain is that the future will be different from today. Rather than trying to predict the future, you must create it if you want to be even remotely in charge of your own destiny. Anticipating commercial and technological events can help you create the future world of Electronic Trading.

We've already seen some results of the effect that new technology can have on our business systems and for example, the Graphical User Interface (GUI) can add a whole new perspective to the "look and feel" of a system by simply exploiting the capability of the humble PC. We discussed earlier how some organisations are exploiting specialist input devices for uses never envisaged when they first emerged, for example, the Dutch farming initiative to use bar-code readers to track their cow population.

But what effect, if any, are technologies such as virtual reality and multimedia going to have on our processes and systems? Will home banking, shopping, and entertainment change our lives as much as the pundits predict? Will you and your workforce be better off if they worked from home rather than taking up valuable office space? Is it more effective to send data electronically to a third world country for processing than to do it in your own company? These are just some of the questions we will have to start asking ourselves and we must be able to understand these issues so that we can evaluate them and decide what the answer should be.

I recently saw an article that drew a parallel between the early industrial revolution infrastructure of canals in England and the "state of the art" electronic infrastructure of today's industry, based on EDI and Value Added Networks. It then postulated on whether, in a hundred years time, we would be building monuments to this ancient electronic infrastructure and have EDI "theme parks" and EDIFACT would be taught as a dead language like Latin and Ancient Greek are today. This may be viewed as flippant, but it's a true indication of the rate of change in technology and the need for us to be able to implement and discard technologies almost at will.

11 Technology moves

This section has probably been the most difficult to write, not just because we don't know what the future holds for technology, although in certain cases this is patently true, but because I don't want to contain future ET applications by focusing your attention on specific technological trends.

I could undoubtedly write a full book on this single topic, but it would extremely boring to read for the majority of people and would still not contain every innovative piece of technology to pass our way over the next few years. So, bear in mind that what I'm about to write gives some examples of technology trends and shouldn't be read as a definitive statement about the immediate, let alone the medium or longer term future. Also remember that a prediction of technology trends has a very short horizon and that anything written on this subject is probably only valid for 5 years (months, weeks, minutes?) at the most.

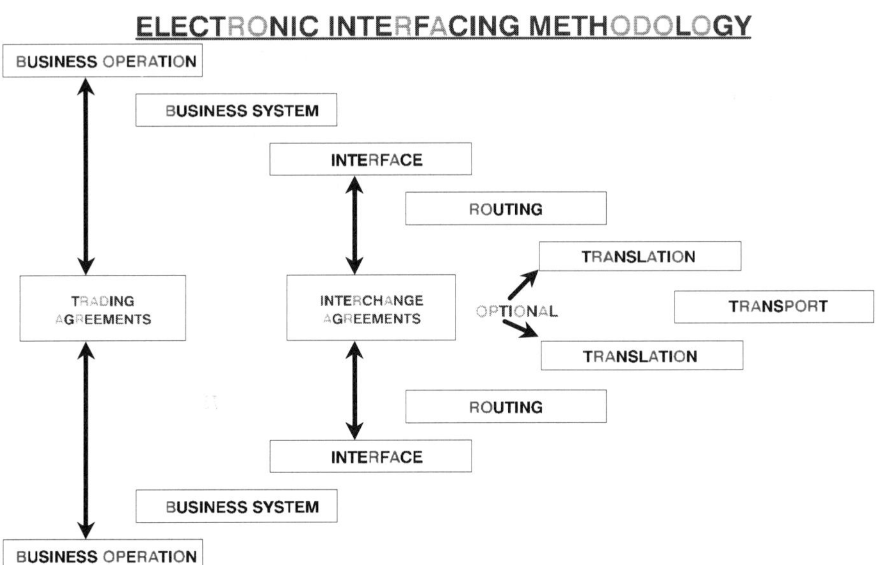

Figure 11-1

In order to review technology in some sort of logical way, I've decided to structure this chapter around the component parts of an electronic link (see Figure 11-1) and hence I'll review Business Systems, Application Development, Standards, Messaging, Networking and Workstations separately.

In each of the sections, I'll simply list some of the relevant technology trends and then briefly discuss the likely impact they'll have - I will leave you to agree, disagree or simply ponder.

It is important to remember though that we must start to view the components of an electronic trading link as cogs of a well-oiled machine and not as an amorphous mass of disparate entities. I have merely separated the components in this section to provide some sort of categorisation of them, not to demonstrate that they should be considered in isolation.

11.1 Business Systems

It is true to say that almost none of the business systems of today have been developed with electronic trading in mind. Some have been developed to distribute information electronically, but very few support a business process that has been designed to work electronically. We still have a paper based business world and it's going to take a long time to change this.

For example, the ATM at the bank still gives us a paper receipt and credit card transactions generate a paper copy; both as a result of our need to have something to audit and record the transaction, but this could be done electronically. Also, E-mail is one of the few business applications that has come about to support an electronic process, but how many people print E-mails to read them? This is caused not so much by the limitations of the system, but restrictions in current desk-top technology - it is easier to digest a document on paper that on screen and also, we mainly like to digest them off-line, at home, on the train, etc. When we get screens that allow us to view a document effectively and on-line, and are sufficiently portable to allow us to carry them around with us wherever we go, then printing of E-mails may be a thing of the past.

Customer Access Terminals

With advances in technology, we should begin to see more evidence of customer access terminals and the bank ATM is a good example of this. The ATM now allows us to get the majority of our banking services from the "hole in the wall". From its early days as a simple cash dispenser, we have seen its functionality enhanced to provide paying in services, statement requests and I would expect these services to continue to grow. In the next chapter, I'll be discussing the advent of interactive television as an example of the new style of customer access terminal.

Electronic Catalogues and other specialised applications

Business systems written specifically with ET in mind will start to emerge. A number of companies, including my own, are producing systems such as Electronic Catalogues that are designed not only to enable customers to electronically identify the product or service they want, but also to order electronically at the point of sale.

Desktop video conferencing

Video conferencing has been used by a number of larger companies since the late 1980s, but the most limiting factor to this facility, ignoring the cost aspect, is that it must be carried out in a specially designed studio that contains the ISDN link to support to voice and picture transmission that enables us to hold business meetings electronically between remote locations. The concept of video conferencing has largely been overtaken by the increased power that people are getting at the desk top that has reached such a level that we now expect to be able to do everything from our office, even "meet" people in remote locations. The technology exists to provide networked ISDN to the desk, and video conferencing workstations are now available that will soon provide the ability to exploit this capability at the desk.

Multimedia enabled systems

Multimedia, as the name implies is the coming together of a number of different technologies for various types of electronic objects, and products will continue to emerge as these technologies mature. We will be able to build systems that manipulate not just textual information, but also moving and of course still pictures, sound, graphics and probably many more we haven't even thought of yet. These products will then start to enable us to build systems where the concept of a document loses all its paper connotations. A "document" comprising of text, image, sound etc., will no longer be suitable for reproducing on paper, it will have to be created, stored and processed totally electronically.

Geographical Information Systems (GIS) is one of the early applications of an information system where the information isn't pure text. Public utilities and government organisations are now starting to see the potential of these systems for managing their asset bases. However, GIS has potential in a whole host of industries, not least, in logistics and distribution, emergency services, postal and delivery services, and the military organisations, who can all exploit the ability to capture and process geographical information.

Expert systems

Artificial Intelligence, Expert and Knowledge-based systems have had a rather chequered history, but this was predominantly caused by the cost and limitations in the technology to deliver them and our inability to recognise that people trained to build traditional functional-based commercial applications are not necessarily the same people you need to build the rule-based systems of the future. As technology continues to advance and we train people in the skills needed to build expert systems and system components, we may start to see more examples such as:-

- Business Insight Software's PC-based system that enables companies to evaluate their business strategy using rules gleaned from 40 world experts on this subject.

- ICL's rules-based computer system configuration tool.
- The Automobile Association's intelligent workstation for validating insurance quotations.

The application for this type of system are endless:- medical diagnosis, law court sentencing, computer based learning, and so on.

Executive information systems

Executive Information Systems (EIS) similarly have not had the best of press over the recent years, but with advances in technology and our ability to harness it, we will be able to deliver EIS systems with simple to use, graphical user interfaces that provide the senior managers with the information they need to take their key decisions.

11.2 Application Development

The tools and methods being used to build our present business systems are largely supportive of traditional functionally oriented systems.

Process capture, analysis, enactment

Business systems of tomorrow will be aligned more to the business process than to specific functional areas and Business Process capture and Analysis tools will continue to advance, with work flow management or process enactment tools being used to build these process aligned systems.

Application Programming Interfaces

Application Programming Interfaces (APIs), which enable applications to interface with the messaging infrastructure, will continue to be developed and agreed. These will then help your internal and external software suppliers generate the right format interfaces, use electronic directory services such as X.500 and ease connection to electronic transport services like X.400. They will also enable us to incorporate open system management techniques to ensure that a distributed system comprising of disparate components spread over multiple disparate hardware platforms, can be managed as though it was resident on a single box. APIs will also facilitate open transaction management by alleviating the current problems of linking to different networks, databases and operating systems.

Mail enabled applications

Mail Enabled Applications (MEAs), under exploited at present, will be necessary to build the workflow systems mentioned above using these standard APIs. We discussed earlier that systems must present output in the format that the user requires and incorporating E-mail connections into business systems is one way of achieving this. For example, a spreadsheet or report generated by the business system can be delivered to a user's electronic mailbox and can then be extracted into an office system for further processing electronically.

Application development tools

Application development tools are needed now more than ever before, as the systems we will be expected to build become ever more complex. We have already discussed how CASE tools have been subject to problems because of standards and we need these tools, and hence the standards for them, to be freely available. We must start to evaluate Computer Aided Software Testing (CAST) products because proving an open, distributed business system works, will be far more complicated than testing one that is single-platform based. In addition to the complexity of the systems, CASE and CAST tools are necessary to increase the productivity of our system building capability.

11.3 Standards

Business objects (Text, EDI, Image etc)

Standards in the "traditional" areas of ET (EDI and E-mail) will continue to advance and become less ambiguous and the use of EDI over X.400 (the X.435 standard) will start to take over from traditional Value Added Network solutions.

The US CALS programme is likely to drive forward the standards work on other electronic objects (graphics, text, image etc.) and the electronic interchange of these objects will then start to take off as the resultant standards become ratified for international use.

Multimedia is one area that will suffer in the same way that CASE has over the years, if standards are not ratified for the range of electronic objects we need to encapsulate in these systems. For example, at the last count, there were thirteen different standards for CD-ROM formats on the market - this must become one single agreed standard.

System Development

Standards in the application system development area will also have a major impact on the way we build systems and CASE tools will begin to become common place when CDIF or an alternative is ratified. Open transaction management will become a reality if the suppliers of products for transaction process monitoring, database access, application development tools and system management start to adopt the OSI Transaction Processing standard.

System Management

Open system management will be vital for our open, distributed systems of the future, but again we need to address the current issue of multiple standards. If this is to be resolved, we need agreement on whether the Internet management (SNMP), the OSI management (CMIP) or the Distributed Management Environment (DME) framework is to be **the** standard for the future.

11.4 Messaging

Standards and implementations for X.400 and the X.500 Directory service will become more mature and X.400 and X.500 products and services will start to proliferate.

Security of messaging systems also relies on standards and already we have the ISO 9796 standard for digital signatures and the X.509 recommendation for user authentication.

Messaging products and services will also begin to cater for all electronic trading objects and not be specific to certain kinds.

We have failed miserably to exploit the capability of X.400 and X.500 and only recently has the UK Ministry of Agriculture Fisheries and Food (MAFF) announced that it is to install one of the first X.500 directories in Europe in order to streamline its E-mail service and enable them to overcome the incompatibilities of messaging system directories. This type of network and messaging capability has so much potential that we can't afford to continue to under-exploit them.

11.5 Networking

The area of networking is liable to be the biggest influence on the advancement (or otherwise) of ET and with this, you must consider whether it is worth building your own private corporate network or buy the service from an external supplier. The Wide Area Networks of today are relatively simple and hence easy to maintain within the larger companies, but as these networks become more complex, you should reconsider this strategy.

With the advent of client-server systems, the network becomes the life-blood of a company's information systems.

Faster communications with more capacity

(High speed X.25, Frame Relay, ATM, SDMS, CDBS)

Faster communication with far greater capacity than current networks is set to come about through broadband technologies such as high speed X.25, frame relay, ATM, SDMS and CDBS. ISDN has not yet been exploited to its full potential and we have seen the service providers waiting for products and the product providers waiting for the service capability.

This scenario will change as the customers start to place the requirement on the service providers for more bandwidth capability and move away from the situation whereby a solution is trying to find a problem to solve. Applications such as in-store electronic catalogues will demand the capability to move sound and image around our networks.

Wireless communications

The advent of wireless communications will stop the need for expensive building cabling projects and provide us with far more flexibility in telecommunications.

Standards on TV Transmission (D-Mac & Digital Signals)

Standards on non-IT technologies, for example television, will help multimedia applications to become established, but we must avoid the dangers of our failure to reach a consensus agreement on the standard for these objects. We all remember the problems caused to both customers and suppliers when domestic video recorders first came to market and three standards (VHS, Betamax and Video 2000) were in use before VHS finally surfaced as the overall winner - a similar issue nearly came about on standards for stereo television, but thankfully the NICAM standard won the battle early.

Video & Desk Top Conferencing

Video conferencing will continue to exploit the ISDN technology, but desk top conferencing will come about as soon as affordable network capacity is extended.

Network integration and interworking

Network integration and interworking will take place as companies recognise the need to create the electronic business network capable of transporting any electronic objects necessary to support the business. The major EDI network operators have failed to interconnect their networks in the past, even though their customers have been demanding it, and only recently have they agreed in principle that this will now happen.

However, network integration goes beyond the simple interconnection of networks for similar electronic objects and the operators must recognise the requirement to transport any type of object. The US's "data super highway" and Europe's "nervous system" initiatives are just two examples that government agencies are taking this requirement very seriously. The Clinton administration in America has allocated some $5 billion over the next four years towards software and hardware development for this type of information highway. Advances in CD-ROM based networks have brought together AT&T's telecommunications, MCA's music, arcades and theme parks, and Time/Warner's publishing businesses and the US Vice-president Al Gore suggests that multimedia networks will be one of the most lucrative marketplaces of the 21st century.

The need for electronic business networks referred to by the MIT90s programme is here today and it is only through exploiting the new telecommunications technologies will we be in a position to make them a reality. Colgate, for example, now has a European network capable of distributing information electronically between all its European sites, but this has only been possible by standardising on Local Area Networks, support systems and office systems and services. This facility has obviously given Colgate tremendous benefit in standardisation of access to their information. The (open) electronic business network, I would suggest though, should not mandate this level of standardisation in local systems and services.

Networking will also expand to cover equipment other than traditional computer-related machines and this is becoming apparent by the work that companies like Microsoft, Rank-Xerox, Ricoh and others are doing on integrating office equipment with personal computers.

External gateways

One aspect of networking that must be considered for the electronic business network is the subject of gateways. Many large companies (such as ICL, BP, Texas Instruments) have implemented corporate gateways to the outside world for EDI and E-mail. The advantage to this approach is that your trading partners see you as a corporate entity rather than a group of separate companies or divisions, but that may not always be what you want. Gateways should also be considered for ALL external electronic traffic: Fax, voice, image, etc.

Neural networks

Neural networks that imitate the human brain, at least to the level that we understand the brain, are not a futuristic pipe dream. This type of network is already demonstrating potential for specific tasks such as matching fingerprints, recognising car number plates and reading text, but their full potential is still to be reached.

11.6 Workstations

Laptop and Portable Computers

The continuing advances in personal computers will increase the power available at the desktop whilst decreasing the amount of space they take up. Portable workstations with docking devices at the desk will be the norm, allowing people the flexibility to move around geographically whilst being able (via the docking device) to transfer information from the portable workstation to and from the corporate network and systems.

Multimedia terminals

Workstations will be capable of presenting and processing the multimedia documents of tomorrow and already devices such as Logitech's handheld scanner, the ScanMan EasyTouch, enable us to input pictures and graphics in addition to Optical Character Recognition (OCR) to our PCs.

Voice and handwriting recognition

Handwriting and voice recognition will change our concepts of the present day terminal and will revolutionise the systems of tomorrow. Pen computers and touch screens will exploit these advances the keyboard may soon go the way of the punched card, for those of you who remember what that was. We will have more capability from our desktop to access other office equipment as the links to Fax machines, telephony services and even the humble photocopier with its new translation facilities.

Multi-function workstations

Multi-function workstations, referred to as Personal Digital or Data Assistants (PDAs), are a result of the amalgamation of office systems, Laptop computers, calculators, telephones and personal organisers and will give us the (portable) capability to take our office wherever it is needed.

11.7 Summary

Different aspects of technology move at different speeds and will never be synchronised. When the network is capable of supporting the new multimedia technologies then the workstations will start to struggle. It's always been like this and is unlikely to change in the future.

Never wait for that new piece of technology that is just round the corner, because by the time it arrives, there will be another more attractive piece round the next corner.

The secret is to make sure that you can intercept new technologies as they come along and don't get locked into any particular one. Open systems architectures are a necessity for the future.

It is now commonplace for company letter heads to contain Fax numbers in addition to telephone numbers and who knows, in the not too distant future, they may all show X.400 E-mail addresses instead - some do already. Indeed Eurodollar has recently replaced telex numbers on its letterheads by X.400 E-mail addresses.

If you "firewall" each system component, replacing old technology by new is far easier.

12 Commercial moves

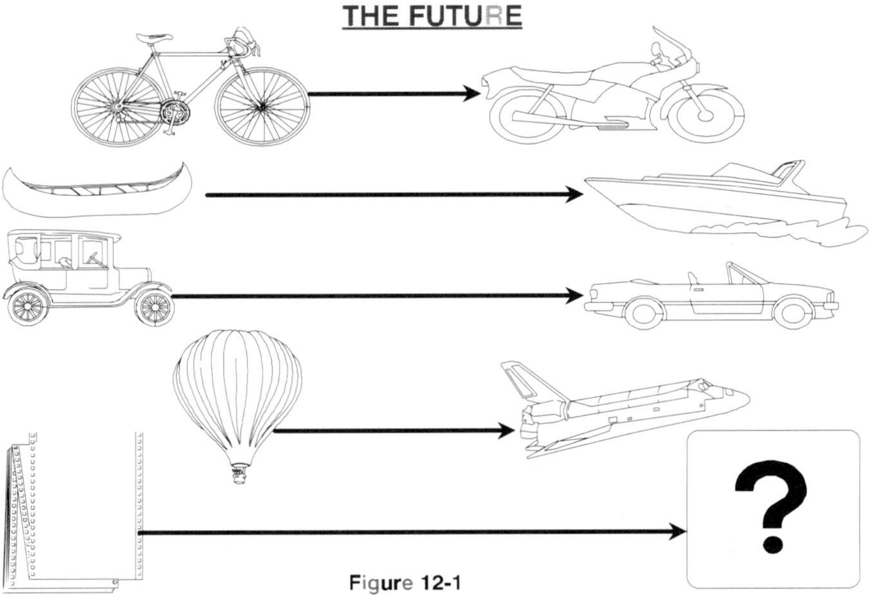

Figure 12-1

There is no doubt that the world has changed as a result of "doing business electronically", consider bank cash points, point of sale equipment, the "humble" PC, office systems, computer based training, etc., etc. These technologies have already made substantial changes to our personal lives, positive improvements for businesses, such as teleworking that allows people to work from home, but there are some more negative aspects to these changes, for example computerised pornography. In this section, I will take a few examples of how electronic business has changed and is continuing to change our world and try to suggest further advances yet to come.

Some of the benefits now being claimed as a direct result of ET or where it at least played a part, are quite spectacular. Take for example:-

- In Germany, the Deutsche Bundespost Postdienst has saved DM14.2 million in time and travel costs during the first four months of its multimedia training project.
- In the UK, Zanussi has increased sales (up by 30% over 3 years) and boosted brand awareness and market share by using interactive POS in nearly 600 white goods stores.
- In Denmark, the estate agency, Home, has increased its market share from 15 to 23 since installing a new ET system.
- In US Sears Roebuck expects to make annual savings of $50 million by using POS systems and interactive multimedia ordering kiosks.
- Zeneca (ICI's pharmaceutical, agrochemical and specialities business division) has reduced its time to market for drugs from 3 years to 14-15 months.

There are also the companies who have found it far from easy to come to terms with some of the new technologies. I was quite amused recently when one of the UK EDI VAN service providers reported that they were having great difficulty implementing electronic Invoicing into their own company. They're now starting to realise that simple service provision isn't sufficient to make ET a reality, but it will help their customers as they begin to come to terms with taking their own medicine and improve their services accordingly.

12.1 A day in the (electronic) life of..."

Rise at 06:30 in a hotel somewhere to the sound of the telephone that automatically rings after being programmed last night. After a quick shower, turn the TV on for an update on yesterday's closing share prices on teletext, then down to breakfast. After breakfast, it's off to reception and check the computer generated, itemised bill (which even tells me I had too much from the bar last night) and pay by credit card, so no cash needed.

On the way to the office, stop off for petrol and again use the trusty plastic card to pay, then a quick stop at the bank to pick up some cash from the cash point machine (yes there are still some places that won't take anything else - the pub etc.) - I can't remember the last time I saw the inside of my bank.

Arrive at work and first thing is to check my E-mail from last night - loads of items to read later, but some urgent items that need replying to. Then it's off to the first meeting, a video conference link to one of our overseas offices. Back from the meeting in time to prepare some slides on the PC and distribute them on E-mail to one of our external service suppliers for his views and comments, before a quick lunch.

After lunch, it's time to check the E-mail situation again and there's one from the european EDI user group giving the agenda for the next meeting in Brussels. Confirm attendance, then Fax the hotel via E-mail from my office system to confirm the reservation, send an E-mail to the travel office to book the flights and one to our director to get Overseas Travel Authorisation. Need to organise a meeting to discuss our messaging network and after checking attendee's availability on the meeting scheduler, send the invitation out with a calendar entry for the meeting. Add a reminder to the system for me to prepare a presentation the week before and then there's just time to download the slides for next month's conference presentation to diskette and send them to the bureau for 35mm slide production - I must find time to write the justification for the equipment to link the PC to the overhead projector. Copy the spreadsheet with next year's budget on to diskette and I think it's time for home.

Settle down in front of the television and upset the kids by flicking through teletext when they wanted to watch the film. After getting banished from the living room because of these anti-social television habits, I upset another of the kids by throwing him off the PC because I need to update the spreadsheet I brought home from work on disc. I just can't win today, anyway while I've commandeered the PC, I can do some more work on that damn book I'm writing and later (much later), it's time for bed - I'm certainly not going to connect to work again to check those flaming E-mails.

This isn't fiction, it's a typical day in the life of the author and when I think back a mere five years, it's exhilarating how much change there's been in that short time. Just imagine what the next five years could bring.

My employers are now making extensive use of Computer Based Training (CBT) within our training division, Peritas and other companies similarly are starting to exploit this capability. For example, I read recently of a company that is using CBT to train their auditors in recognising misuse of computer systems.

We also make use of knowledge based systems in a number of our divisions, multimedia technology for the release of technical manuals, EDI and E-mail both internally and with our external trading partners, bar-coding for tracking goods and fixed assets, exchange of 2 and 3 dimensional drawings with our component suppliers, electronic business forms and we have plans for far more as you will see from the case study later.

Companies are definitely recognising the need to trade electronically in everything they do and to some extent are being hampered by the slowness of the standardisation work.

12.2 The changing face of commerce

Home Shopping

BSkyB launched the first UK home shopping channel in October 1993 where customers select goods via the TV, phone in and pay by credit card. However, the service will only be available to 10% of the homes in UK and mail order catalogues already have a big hold on the market, so will it be successful?

Home shopping services have been prevalent in US for some

time, but they are now moving to "interactive shopping" - for example, you watch your favourite soap and order items seen during the programme (furniture, clothes etc.), all on-line. The broadcaster can "invade" your home:- real-time surveys during chat shows, consumer specific advertising (why send you details of a Rolls Royce when they know you can only afford a Lada) - the list is endless.

Success in the UK will be influenced by the current hold of mail order and may simply put some of the smaller catalogues out of business. Take up will also be influenced by the UK geography - as we are much smaller than the US and have a good infrastructure of out-of-town superstores, there may not be the market demand for home shopping. Furthermore, if interactive TV catches on in the US, then the older technology of home shopping may be difficult to sell in the UK

Publishing

At the beginning of the book, I mentioned the improvements to our office facilities during the last 5 years and how it was possible to despatch an electronic copy of this manuscript, albeit on diskette, to the publisher. Let's now take this a stage further and look at what improvements can still be made to this process, even with today's technology.

The first improvement is obviously to despatch the finished manuscript by E-mail to the publishers, which is no problem even today. Next, the publisher and author could use desk-top conferencing to interactively agree final amendments to the document before committing to "print". Yes, I say "print" but don't assume that it's a paper document I refer to, the finished article could just as easily be made available on CD-ROM, diskette or even via E-mail. However, to make some of these possible, the copyright and royalty positions need to be reviewed, as a document issued by E-mail can be simply replicated and distributed widely.

Electronic Catalogue Sales

Imagine the trip to your local do-it-yourself store, which may be a real store or simply another service via the TV. You browse through the electronic catalogue and decide which bathroom suite you want having seen a full colour image of it. Want some help in fitting it? Sure, the system is there to help and can give you a 10 minute video presentation of helpful tips.

Need to know what fixtures and fittings you need, all the options are listed, just point and click on all the items you want, key in your debit card number and the order is taken and delivery date confirmed.

Customer satisfaction is assured and the "store" doesn't need vast stocks of items for people to look at. Argos stores in the UK have already been very successful at minimising their in-store stock by the use of paper catalogues, but with electronic catalogues you can not only minimise your in-store stocks, you can also effectively extend your range of merchandise without the need to build stock.

Think of buying a house - using a similar catalogue system, you enter your selection criteria (5 bedrooms, 3 bathrooms......) and the system takes over. Three properties are short listed in the area you selected, now sit back and be taken on a guided tour of each as the video rolls and you start to make your selection. This scenario is not far off reality when you look at what Homevision, the Danish estate agent's system has achieved in the last three years. Using touch screens, you select the area in which you want to live, the type of home you want, how much you can afford to pay and the system displays all the properties that match your criteria. The system provides textual information, pictures (internal and external), floor plans, a map of the area and can even provide an audio guide so that you don't need the estate agent breathing down your neck.

The music industry is also starting to catch on to this capability and already, Polygram, BMG and EMI have established EROS

Ltd (Electronic Record Ordering music System) which now covers 60% of the UK market and are currently looking at the shop front ordering process, where electronic catalogues may be the answer.

Electronic Catalogue potential just goes on and on:- video rental, job centres....... The point is that it is one of the few electronic trading systems in existence.

12.3 The business of tomorrow

There's nothing more certain than the businesses of tomorrow will work differently than those of today. The ones who survive will be those who can and will change.

Manufacturing

The manufacturing industry has already seen tremendous change caused by technology (robotics, computerisation etc.) brought about by the ever demanding need to make things quicker and at less cost. Productivity in most areas of the industry has risen dramatically since the Second World War and continues to rise as foreign competitors put pressure on one another by finding cheaper methods of manufacturing. Electronic business will be a major factor in the next round of productivity improvements as standards for text, image etc., start to get ratified.

Deregulation

Deregulation of trading restrictions will bring about many more changes. Consider the way ET is taking off in India as a result of the relaxation of the international trading restrictions. This relaxation has lead to foreign investors and multi-national companies moving into India and hence an upturn in the need for ET. The government of India's telecommunications enterprise VSNL (Videsh Sanchar Nigan Ltd) is now set to launch an EDI service GEDIS (Gateway Electronic Document Interchange Service) based on INS's TRADANET service.

Retail

More and more industry sectors are turning to EDI following the early lead shown by the Retail industry and although EDI has been in use for the last decade, take up has been very slow and has been forced in by the larger ("hub") companies. EDI will continue to grow as the companies who have now invested in it start to encourage their trading partners to use it, who in turn will then encourage their trading partners, and so on.

Financial services and retail have both benefited from the advances in workstation and networking technologies, but will now have to fight a rear-guard action against the telesales and home-shopping operators.

Travel

The travel industry has been at the forefront of electronic trading for a number of years and yet their rate of progress appears to have slowed down. This is in some part due to the amount of work needed simply to "stand still" in IT systems, but can they afford this luxury when the world's population increasingly views the world as a smaller place and wants to travel further afield at lower cost? The customer will want to order travel facilities in a simpler and more easy manner than today - and pay less for it.

Construction

Construction has felt the impact of Computer Aided Design, but needs to take more advantage of some of the other aspects of electronic business technology to improve its productivity during the coming years. Control of its subcontractors for example could be greatly improved by electronic communications.

Motor Trade

The motor trade has exploited technology, but this has predominantly been on the manufacturing side. Retailing of automotive products and services can still benefit greatly from ET techniques. Electronic catalogues would greatly improve the services offered within the car showrooms and spares departments.

Changing Commercial Processes

We must also consider our commercial processes and question the validity of some of the practices that, let's face it, have their origins back in the days of the industrial revolution. For example, why do we need to raise invoices when the customer can initiate payment as soon as the goods are received - i.e. self-billing? Another example could be orders; as the customer and supplier relationship becomes closer, why can the customer not just provide stock and forecast information for the supplier to calculate what he needs and when he needs it? We have the ability to radical change some of the less efficient and bureaucratic processes that were designed for paper-based systems.

Trends

Consider also some of the general trends now becoming apparent which will potentially change the way we do business:-

- More intelligent, knowledge based, IT systems will continue to take the drudgery out of all industries and automate more and more processes. A trivial example is the grammar checking capability of our word processing systems, which now ensure that not only is the spelling correct but our grammar is improved as well.
- Home working, or Teleworking, will become more the norm than of late, as a result of improvements in IT and telephony products and services.
- The days of the full-time job for the majority of the population may become a thing of the past as companies move towards the virtual organisation.
- "Expert" systems will capture specialist knowledge and help to provide continuity in volatile organisations in addition to enhancing the services of doctors, lawyers, etc.

- Voice recognition systems will bring productivity increases far beyond our traditional keyboard technologies.
- Computerised guidance systems and road charging will revolutionise our traffic and distribution sectors. The system of on-board computers on trial in Boston, USA provides the driver with information on the location of the cheapest petrol in the area when it detects that the vehicle needs more fuel.
- Vehicle and goods tracking systems exploiting satellite communications are already being introduced by telecommunication service operators in conjunction with logistics companies.
- Virtual Reality systems are currently being used for games applications, but just consider their benefit for product design and prototyping. If you could actually see a proposed new product in "real life" the savings would be colossal.
- We have already discussed Geographical Information Systems, but like virtual reality, do we really understand their potential for commercial applications. I have previously suggested that they have potential for vehicle tracking, emergency services, postal and delivery services, but what other potential is there for these systems?

I hope by now you are starting to doubt my sanity and saying "no this is the way it's going to be". I don't have all the answers, but I do have a lot of questions and if by asking these questions I can start you thinking about the way it will be, then we will begin to move forward.

The only thing certain about the future is that it will be different - so let's not assume we will be doing business the same way we have for the last century.

Part 5

Summary and Conclusions

*"Electronic Trading", "Electronic Commerce", Electronic Business", "Doing Business Electronically" - whatever you call it, be clear you understand what **YOU** mean by it.*

Throughout the book, I have been advocating that ET involves the electronic interchange of any object of a business transaction using mutually (preferably International) agreed standards and covers trading in its most catholic sense:- interpersonal, system to system and people to and from systems. You may disagree, but whatever you decide ET means, it's important that both you and your trading partners agree the same definition and scope.

Summary and Conclusions

My perspective of ET has been derived from the experience I've had within an International IT company, but I have tried to write this book with all shapes and sizes of company in mind, in any industry grouping and hence I hope that all readers will find it applicable to their organisation, big or small, national or international. The principles I've laid down apply equally to internal trading partners as to external ones and multi-divisional companies should find this useful.

If I've any one single message to end this book on it's simply

> **"To ignore ET in today's turbulent world is to bury your head in the sand - to do so, is to risk the future survival of your business"**.

It isn't some management consultant's fashion that will go away tomorrow, it's here to stay and is the way we will be doing business tomorrow, continuing to improve the productivity and viability of our organisations. At the very least, you need an ET strategy today that will take you through to the next decade.

This point was underwritten by David Garrett, Comag's MD (independent distributor owned by National Magazine Company [She & Cosmopolitan] and Conde Nast [Vogue & Home and Garden] when he said that the 1990s need a different approach in publishing philosophy compared with the paper-profligate 1980s. He then went on to say that there will be a growing emphasis on title range management by both wholesale and retail trades. Information about marketplace and product performance will not merely be critical but a 'sine qua non' - those companies that cannot supply the information needs of the rest of the industry will die. This message applies to the whole of industry, not just to the publishing companies. The message was also stated by Sir John

Harvey-Jones at a recent ET conference when he said that there is no way of having sustainable competitive advantage through IT, but that you can sure as hell get sustainable disadvantage by not being up with the best in IT.

I have tried to write the book to suit readers in all walks of commercial life, from the senior manager to the system developer, which was always a tall order given this span of audience, but I trust that all of you have got at least something out of it. I've also tried to keep it technology free, but inevitably techno-speak was necessary in certain places and I hope that the glossary helps overcome any confusion.

The benefits section in Part 1 indicated**some** of the gains you can expect from this way of doing business, but wherever possible, I tried to position case study material in the most appropriate sections and hopefully this gave additional insight into what is possible.

The Management in the Nineties and History sections in Chapters 3 and 4 indicated that ET is high on the agenda of the business gurus and is nothing new - we just have more appropriate technology today and will have even more appropriate technology tomorrow.

In Chapter 5 I attempted to list the "blockers" or excuses that I've come across for not addressing ET. You obviously have to be aware of these, but don't lose sleep over them because they aren't real problems, just obstacles you'll have to overcome. I always remember, a number of years ago now, a manufacturing company I was working for at that time tried to persuade its shop floor workers to move from cash payment to bank transfer and the excuses for not doing so were numerous and mostly fictional. The real reason, was that they didn't want their wives to find out how much they earned and if it was paid directly to the bank, it would be more difficult to hide this. Once we had established this root cause of their reticence, we could start to address it - so don't necessarily believe the initial fears and concerns expressed are the real problems.

Part 3 was, what I consider to be, the most important section of the book, looking at the real problems of implementing ET projects and programmes, from the people and culture aspects (Chapter 6), commercial considerations (Chapter 7), standards and infrastructure (Chapter 8), system development (Chapter 9) and finally implementation management (Chapter 10). The conclusion you will have noted from this section is that it isn't going to be easy to implement, because it involves a number of diverse organisations and disciplines, but with the right management it's by no means impossible.

In the final section I dusted down my crystal ball and tried to predict the future for both the technological and commercial aspects of ET, but the primary objective was to be as controversial as possible and get you to question my theories. It's fun to look at what's round the corner, but don't lose sight of the transitional issue of how you get from where you are today to where you know you want to be tomorrow. There are always going to be the issues when we look at introducing new technologies and the current problem of the relatively high cost of CD-ROM manufacture as opposed to the low price that the predominantly domestic market will bear is a good example of how pricing can dictate market take up. Also, some of the other technological innovations such as virtual reality are simply not understood yet for us to realise their true potential. But these are temporary hold-ups rather than show stoppers.

Some of the changes in our organisations today are tremendously exciting and encouraging for the more strategic thinkers and when we witness previously competitive companies working together for the common good, this can only be viewed as excellent news. Take for example the oil industry project JIBE (Joint Industry Billing Exchange) initiated by BP, Mobil and Shell. Also, the work being done in Finland by ICL, IBM, Compaq, HP and Canon who are working together to provide EDI services.

I sincerely hope that you have both enjoyed the book and found it, in some slight way, educational and if my experiences help you to carry out an easier ET programme as a result of reading this, then it will have all been worthwhile. I hope you can now ask the right questions, of the right people to get the answers to your problems.

Any feedback on your ET experiences and the value, or otherwise, of this book would be most gratefully received - let's trade (electronically of course). My E-mail address can be found at the end of the Introduction section.

THE BENEFITS OF ET

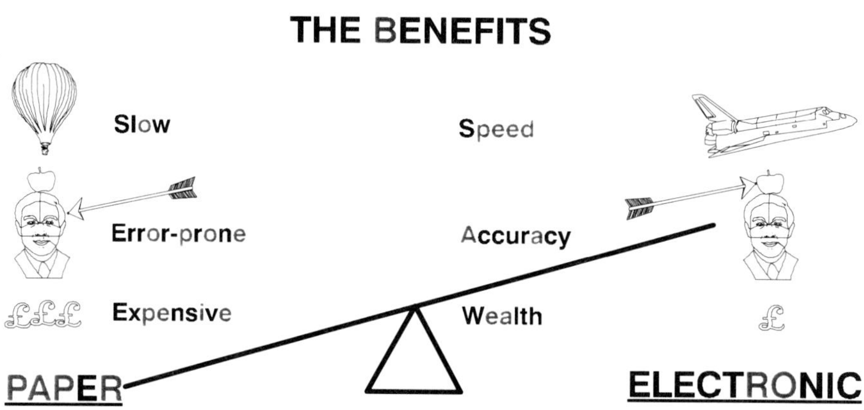

Figure 13-1

"Everything except hardware and people will be distributed electronically" is ICL's ET vision and continues to improve the efficiency and effectiveness of the organisation.

It can do the same for your organisation.

Appendices

A Useful addresses

ANA (UK) Ltd Tel: +44 71 240 2874 Fax: +44 71 240 8149	11 Kingsway LONDON WC2B 6AR
AUSTRIAPRO Tel: +43 1 50105 Fax: +43 1 50206250	Wiedner Haupstrasse 63 PO Box 150 A-1045 Wien, Austria
British Computer Society Tel: +44 793 480 269 Fax: +44 793 480 270	PO Box 1454 Station Road, Swindon SN1 1TG UK
CMI Tel: +44 71 924 7117 Fax: +44 71 403 6729	Letts of London House Parkgate Road, London SW11 4NQ UK
Commission of the EC Tel: +32 2 299 02 85 Fax: +32 2 299 02 86	Rue de la Loi 200 B-1049 Brussels Belgium
DANPRO Tel: +45 33 950500 Fax: +45 33 330464	C/O Danish EDI-Council Borsen 1217 Copenhagen K 1217 Denmark
DTI Tel: +44 71 215 1526 Fax: +44 71 215 2909	Technology & Programme Services Division 151 Buckingham Palace Rd London. SW1W 9SS UK

DEUPRO
Tel: +49 228 615 2733
Fax: +49 228 615 4436
Bundesministerium fur
Wirtschaft
53123 Bonn, Germany

The EDIA Association
Tel: +44 71 824 8848
Fax: +44 71 824 8114
148 Buckingham Palace Rd
London. SW1W 9TR
UK

EDI Association of Ireland
Tel: +353 6609532
Fax: +353 6609828
95 Haddington Road
Ballsbridge Dublin 4
Ireland

EDICON
Tel: +44 252 336318
Fax: +44 252 333901
PO Box 111
Aldershot
Hants. GU11 1YW UK

EDICUG
Tel: +44 71 580 6633
c/o Phillips Components
Mullard House
Torrington Place
London. WC1E 7HD UK

EDIFICE
Tel: +32 2 538 7421
Fax: +32 2 539 3641
c/o AST
Avenue Du Roi 191
1060 Brussels, Belgium

EDIFORUM
Tel: +31 70 3376111
Fax: +31 70 3276965
p/a Stichting Sociaal
Fonds Bouwnijverhd
PO Box 262
NL-2260 AG Leidschendam
Netherlands

EDIFRANCE
Tel: +33 1 42 91 57 93
Fax: +33 1 42 91 60 26
Tour Europe - Cedex 7
92049 Paris la Defense
France

EDISHIP
Tel: +44 81 507 8486

PO Box 52
Barking
Essex. IG11 7HB UK

EDIS
Tel: +46 8 793 90 06
Fax: +46 8 751 53 63

Electrum 228
S-164 40 Kista
Sweden

EEMA
Tel: +44 386 793028
Fax: +44 386 793268

Executive Office
Pastoral House
Ramble Close, Inkberrow
Worcester. WR7 4EL
UK

Electronic Trader
Tel: +44 769 580246
Fax: +44 769 581045

1 New Street
Chulmleigh
Devon. EX18 7DB UK

EOLAS
Tel: +353 1 370101
Fax: +353 1 379620

Glassnevin
Dublin 9
Ireland

Finnish Data Communication Association
Tel: +358 0 685 1312
Fax: +358 0 685 1616

Salomonkatu 17A
10th Floor
Helsinki 00100
Finland

HUNPRO
Tel: +36 1 131 8958
Fax: +36 1 131 8958

Ministry of International Economic Relations
Honved u. 13-15
H-1880 Budapest
Hungary

ICL Tel: +44 782 771000 Fax: +44 782 776667	EnterpriseSystems Electronic Business Unit Westfields, West Avenue Kidsgrove, Stoke-on-Trent Staffordshire. UK
IPS Tel: +44 780 56777	Easton House Easton on the Hill Stamford, Lincolnshire PE9 3NZ UK
National Computing Centre Tel: +44 61 228 6333 Fax: +44 61 237 1636	Oxford House Oxford Road Manchester. M17ED UK
NORPRI Tel: +47 2 557032 Fax: +47 2 552362	PO Box 2526 Solli N-0203 Oslo 2, Norway
ODETTE Tel: +44 71 235 7000 Fax: +44 71 235 7112	SMMT, Forbes House Halkin Street, London. SW1X 7DS UK
POLPRO Tel: +48 22 266 065 Fax: +48 22 276 810	Foundation for Polish Export, Kvolewska 27 Warsaw 00 060, Poland
Royal Mail Tel: +44 71 250 2332 Fax: +44 71 250 2469	76 Turnmill Street London. EC1M 5NS UK
SIMPROESPANA Tel: +34 91 5639438 Fax: +34 91 2628023	C.E.O.E Diego de Leon 50 28006 Madrid, Spain

SEMPRO ITALIA Tel: +39 6 5993	Ministero per il Commercio Estero Viale America 321 00100 Roma EUR, Italy
SITPRO Tel: +44 71 287 3525 Fax: +44 71 287 5751	29 Glasshouse Street LONDON W1R 5RG
SITPROCOM Tel: +32 2 2194550 Fax: +32 2 2194550	Office Belge du Commerce Exterieur WTC bl. Emile Jacqmain 162 1000 Brussels, Belgium
SWEPRO Kommerskollegium Tel: +46 8 791 0500 Fax: +46 8 200 324	Birger Jarls Torg 5 Box 1209 S-111 82 Stockholm Sweden
SWISSPRO Tel: +41 31 25 58 11	PO Box 1458 CH-30001 Bern Switzerland
UN-ECE Tel: +41 71 22 917 2745 Fax: +41 71 22 917 0036	Trade Division Bureau 450 Palaise de Nations Geneva CH-1210 Switzerland
VideoLogic Tel: +44 923 260511 Fax: +44 923 268969	Home Park Estate Kings Langley Herts. WD4 8LZ UK

Value Added Network Operators

All the following companies operate VAN services across a range of industry groups and countries. I have not attempted to include all suppliers of VANs and VADS for specific industries or geographies.

AT&T Easylink Services
Tel: +44 71 251 1577
Fax: +44 71 253 0416
Melbray House
Bastwick Street
LONDON. EC1V 3PH UK

Brains NV
Tel: +32 2 718 7070
Fax: +32 2 718 7071
Excelsiorlaan 44-46
Zaventern
Belgium

BT
Tel: +44 0800 282444
Network House
Brindley Way
Hemel Hampstead
Herts. HP3 9RR UK

BT France
Tel: +33 1 46 67 23 27
Fax: +33 1 47 68 98 42
Immeurce Jean Monnet
Cedex 56
PARIS. La Defense V
92061. France

CMA Data A/S
Tel: +45 429 188 33
Fax: +45 428 429 50
46B, Marielundveg
DK-2730 Herlev
Denmark

Comlink
Tel: +45 86 28 66 77
Fax: +45 86 28 62 11
Fabrikver 11
8260 Viby
Denmark

Dannet A/S
Tel: +45 45 82 16 00
Fax: +45 45 82 16 44
Blokken 9
Birkeroed
DK 3460, Denmark

EDES Ltd Tel: +44 932 859066 Fax: +44 932 850089	Orion House 49 High Street Addlestone Surrey. KT15 1TU UK
EDS Sweden AB Tel: +46 8 619 1000 Fax: +46 8 656 5200	Box 30194 Stockholm S-104 25 Sweden
ELMA OY Electronic Marketing Tel: +358 0 692 7466 Fax: +358 0 670 156	Wavulinintie 10 Helsinki SF 00210 Finland
EMS-Electronic Marketing Services Tel: +47 22 416666 Fax: +47 22 725286	Rosenkranzgaten 22 0160 Oslo Norway
GE Information Services Tel: +33 1 46 73 16 00 Fax: +33 1 46 73 16 01	19 Ave Leon Gambetta 92120 Montrouge France
GEIS (UK) Ltd Tel: +44 81 741 0077 Fax: +44 81 741 1939	4th Floor, 3 Shortlands Hammersmith, London W6 8BX UK
GSI Tel: +33 1 45 02 74 75 Fax: +33 1 45 00 59 53	25 Boulevard de l'Amiral Bruix 75116 Paris, France

GSI Transport & Touristik Tel: +49 6151 7003 0 Fax: +49 6151 77469	Bartningstrabe 55 64289 Darmstadt or PO Box 10 06 06 Darmstadt 64205, Germany
IBM UK Ltd Tel: +44 256 343085 Fax: +44 256 479366	PO Box 117 Mountbatten House Basing View, Basingstoke Hampshire. RG21 1EJ UK
INS Tel: +44 932 776000 Fax: +44 932 776020	INS House Station Road Sunbury-on-Thames Middlesex. TW16 6SB UK
Landbrugets EDB-Centre (LEC) Tel: +45 86 21 40 00 Fax: +45 86 21 70 05	Bytoften PO Box 2201 DK 8240 Risskov, Denmark
NDC International Tel: +44 71 371 6465 Fax: +44 71 371 2068	Crown House 72 Hammersmith Road London. W14 8YD UK
PostGem Ltd Tel: +353 1 676 8744 Fax: +353 1 676 8727	Alexandra House Earlsfort Centre Earlsfort Terrace Dublin 2, Ireland
PTT Telecom Tel: + 31 70 343 3412 Fax: +31 70 343 7605	Junostraat 35-37 PO Box 30150 2500 GD Gravenwhale Netherlands

Racal Network Services
Tel: +44 0256 700500
Fax: +44 0256 700110

Oakwood
Crockford Lane
Chineham Business Park
Basingstoke, Hampshire
RG24 8WB UK

Responsor A/S
Tel: +45 42 91 88 33
Fax: +45 42 84 29 50

Marielundvej 46B
DK-2730 Herlev
Denmark

Transpac SA
Tel: +33 1 46 48 15 15
Fax: +33 1 46 48 16 16

Tour Montparnasse
33 Avenue du Naive B13
Cedex 15, 75755, France

Vertis BV
Tel: +31 5987 68000
Fax: +31 5987 68092

PO Box 73
Veendam
9640 AB, Netherlands

B Bibliography

Computer Mediated Communication and the Law
Benjamin Wright J.D. in The Matrix-Computer Networks and Conferencing Systems Worldwide - John S Quarterman, Digital Press. ISBN 1-55558-033-5

DIP Applications Handbook
NCC Blackwell. Edited by NCC. ISBN 1-85554-141-6.

Document Interchange - Management Guide
NCC Blackwell / DISC. Richard Carr. ISBN 1-85554-182-3.

EDI - a guide for purchasing and supply managers
An IPS briefing publication. Vaughn Armstrong / David Jackson. ISBN 0-900607-70-X

EDI and the Law
Edited by Ian Walden. NCC Blackwell. ISBN 0-86353-170-9

EDI: Audit and Control
NCC Blackwell. Edited by Ian Walden and Ashley Braganza. ISBN 1-85554-208-0.

EDI Handbook
NCC Blackwell. Edited by M.Gifkins and D.Hitchcock. ISBN 0-86353-148-2.

EDI IT Report
UNICOM Seminars Ltd, Brunel Science Park, Cleveland Road, Uxbridge, Middlesex. UB8 3PH. UK.

EDI Security - Today and Tomorrow
John Williamson / John E Draper, IFIP TC11 International Conference on Information Security 1991. Elsevier Science Publishers BV ISBN 0-444-89219-2

EDI Technology
NCC Blackwell. Edited by M.Gifkins. ISBN 0-86353-204-7.

EDI - What Managers Need to know about the revolution in business communications.
TAB Professional and Reference Books. Richard H Baker.
ISBN 0-8306-7724-O

Electronic Data Interchange and paperless Trading
NCC Blackwell. Blenheim. ISBN 0-86353-240-3

Executive Information Systems
NCC Blackwell. J.Bird. ISBN 0-85012-789-0.

File Transfer Access and Management: A Practical Guide
NCC Blackwell. DISC/DTI. ISBN 1-85554-199-8.

File Transfer Access and Management: A Technical Guide
NCC Blackwell. DISC/DTI. ISBN 1-85554-191-2.

Future Networks
NCC Blackwell. R.Reardon. ISBN 0-86353-163-6.

Handbook of Data Communications
NCC Blackwell. NCC. ISBN 1-85554-002-9.

High Performance Computing
O'Reilly & Associates Inc. Kevin Dowd. ISBN 1-56592-000-7.

Human Computer Interaction
NCC Blackwell. David Steele. ISBN 1-85554-180-7.

Information Security
NCC Blackwell. Michael Brewer. ISBN 1-85554-179-3.

ISDN Applications
NCC Blackwell. I.Benton. ISBN 1-85554-145-9.

Management Guide to CBT Interactive Video
NCC Blackwell. R.Palmer. ISBN 0-85012-674-6.

Message Handling Systems: A Practical Guide
NCC Blackwell. DISC/DTI. ISBN 1-85554-200-5.

Message Handling Systems: A Technical Guide
NCC Blackwell. DISC/DTI. ISBN 1-85554-192-0.

Mobile Data Communications - Choices and Opportunities
NCC Blackwell. A.Jowett. ISBN 1-85554-146-7.

Multimedia Mania
Abacus. ISBN 1-55755-166-9. Also includes CD-ROM with examples.

Network Security
NCC Blackwell. Mario Devargas. ISBN 1-85554-201-3.

Networks for the 1990s
NCC Blackwell. R.Reardon. ISBN 0-86353-13108.

Open Systems - Management Guide
NCC Blackwell. Jack Houldsworth. ISBN 1-85554-181-5.

Open Systems LANs
Butterworth-Heinemann. Jack Houldsworth et al. ISBN 07506 1045 X

***OPEN*framework**: *Availability quality*
Prentice Hall. ICL. ISBN 0-13-630948-8.

***OPEN*framework**: *Usability quality*
Prentice Hall. ICL. ISBN 0-13-630930-5.

***OPEN*framework**: *Performance quality*
Prentice Hall. ICL. ISBN 0-13-630666-7.

***OPEN*framework**: *Security quality*
Prentice Hall. ICL. ISBN 0-13-630658-6.

***OPEN*framework**: *Potential for Change quality*
Prentice Hall. ICL. ISBN 0-13-630617-9.

***OPEN*framework**: *User Interface element*
Prentice Hall. ICL. ISBN 0-13-630591-1.

***OPEN*framework**: *Distributed Application Services element*
Prentice Hall. ICL. ISBN 0-13-630518-0.

***OPEN*framework**: *Information Management element.*
Prentice Hall. ICL. ISBN 0-13-630500-8.

***OPEN*framework**: *Application Development element.*
Prentice Hall. ICL. ISBN 0-13-630484-2.

***OPEN*framework**: *Systems Management element.*
Prentice Hall. ICL. ISBN 0-13-630450-8.

***OPEN*framework**: *Networking Services element.*
Prentice Hall. ICL. ISBN 0-13-630393-5.

***OPEN*framework**: *Platforms element.*
Prentice Hall. ICL. ISBN 0-13-630385-4.

***OPEN*framework**: *Transaction Management specialisation.*
Prentice Hall. ICL. ISBN 0-13-630377-3.

OSI Directory Service: A Practical Guide.
NCC Blackwell. DISC/DTI. ISBN 1-85554-197-1.

OSI Directory Service: A Technical Guide.
NCC Blackwell. DISC/DTI. ISBN 1-85554-189-0.

OSI Management: A Practical Guide.
NCC Blackwell. DISC/DTI. ISBN 1-85554-195-5.

OSI Management: A Technical Guide.
NCC Blackwell. DISC/DTI. ISBN 1-85554-187-4.

OSI Standards and Acronyms.
NCC Blackwell. Compiled by Adrian Stokes. ISBN 1-85554-142-4.

Practical Open Systems - A Guide for Managers.
NCC Blackwell. Data General Ltd. ISBN 1-85554-211-0.

Smart Cards and Memory Cards.
NCC Blackwell. M.Devargas. ISBN 1-85554-139-4.

Strategies for Text Communication.
NCC Blackwell. T.Squires. ISBN 0-85012-790-4.

The Age of Unreason.
Century Business, 1993. Charles Handy. ISBN 0-7126-4931-X.

The Corporation of the 1990s.
Oxford University Press, 1993. Michael Scott Morton. ISBN 0-19-506358-9.

The EDI Implementors' Handbook.
NCC Blackwell. NCC. ISBN 1 85554 161 0.

The EDI yearbook
published annually by Blenheim and NCC Blackwell

The EDIFACT standards.
NCC Blackwell. J.Berge. ISBN 1 85554 070 3

The Legal Position of the Member States with respect to Electronic Data Interchange
Final Report, September 1989 for the TEDIS Programme of the Commission of the European Communities. Law Office of Lopomez, Crouquet.

The Systems Architecture: an Introduction.
Prentice Hall. ICL. ISBN 0-13-560186-X.

The VANS Handbook.
NCC Blackwell. Edited by C.Chang and D.Hitchcock. ISBN 0-86353-179-2.

The Whole Internet User's Guide & Catalog.
O'Reilly & Associates Inc. Ed Krol. ISBN 1-56592-025-2.

Understanding DCE.
O'Reilly & Associates Inc. Ward Rosenberry, David Kenney & Gerry Fisher. ISBN 1-56592-005-8.

What is EDI?
NCC Blackwell. Martin Parfett. ISBN 1 85554 166 1

What is DIP?
NCC Blackwell. M.Parfett. ISBN 1-85554-165-3.

What is OSI?
NCC Blackwell. C.Pye. ISBN 0-85012-642-8.

X.400: The Messaging and Interconnection Medium for the Future.
NCC Blackwell. P.Chilton. ISBN 0-85012-685-1.

C Case study "Why ICL is using ET"

1. Introduction

ICL is a leading, profitable international IT company with operations in over 70 countries world-wide, and a total revenue of 2.6 billion in 1992. ICL's wholehearted adoption and exploitation of electronic trading techniques, particularly our progress in EDI, has recently been recognised by a public award. The International Data Exchange Association, Brussels, and "*EDI, Spread the Word!*" gave ICL the European EDI Leadership Award for the Electronics Industry.

2. Before Electronic Trading

High-technology components form the bulk of ICL's hardware product input. Our component suppliers are located throughout Europe, Asia-Pacific, and North America - and before electronic trading, lead times for new component supplies and final products used to be measured in months. ICL could react to changes in technology and market demand, but only slowly, and intense effort had to be applied to ensure that procurement, production and stocks stayed in line with business needs. Faxs, telephone calls and letters flowed heavily between ICL Purchasing and our suppliers to maintain the necessary level of communication and understanding.

In addition, development of new component designs and turning these into product realities was generally a serial process - exacerbating the overall lead times. As a result, yet more management effort was needed to make sales forecasts as accurate as possible even when made many months in advance, and then to turn these forecasts into real business results.

Hardware and associated ICL software on magnetic media were eventually shipped (often by air) with much paper form-filling and telephone scheduling, to clients around the globe.

Similarly, provision and scheduling of specialist skilled staff (technicians and business consultants) to clients were bedevilled by the vagaries of the forecasting system and product lead times. Backup documentation was available by the ton, the vast majority on paper. And around the world, most of ICL's internal operations were conducted on paper - a very rewarding situation for paper manufacturers and courier companies, but one that limited the synergy possible between Product Development, Marketing, and Country Operations.

3. ICL's Vision

In the late 1980s there was significant management focus on the logistics of supply, improving the forecasting process, allying this to collaborating more closely with our suppliers and beginning to exploit concurrent engineering development techniques.

Out of this work came several major initiatives, including the Vendor Development Programme and ICL's Electronic Trading Vision, which states that "***Everything except hardware and people will be distributed electronically***". These are key aspects of our company-wide drive to be the leading European IT company and "a better company to do business with". The rest of this case study shows the results we have achieved so far, with a spotlight on EDI and electronic mail, and where we are heading in the near future.

4. ICL Now

4.1 Vendor Development Programme

The Vendor Development Programme, aimed at improving the trading relationship between ICL and its key vendors, is now well established and provides benefits to both ourselves and our suppliers. We see suppliers having greater awareness of our requirements, increased involvement in the ICL quality improvement process, and many other benefits, all arising from greater ICL attention and focus on our key vendors. On their part, our vendors gain greater visibility of ICL's forward plans, the right audience for their presentations, the opportunity to take part in our manufacturing planning, and access to ICL's skilled staff and techniques in addressing new or problematical product or business situations. Underpinning this programme is our dedication to trading with our vendors electronically - in line with ICL's ET vision.

4.2 Trading by EDI

We currently have in excess of 150 of our major suppliers using EDI, assisted by an Electronic Trading Team. These companies account for some 60% of our Purchase Order trading, and the percentage is rising every month. This rise is accompanied by a corresponding decline in the number of Faxes, phone calls and general paper mail. 99% of our export freight bookings are managed by EDI, speeding up our deliveries to customers and greatly reducing the hassle of our being a major exporter - 60% of ICL's revenue now comes from outside the UK.

Internally, orders from ICL operating companies as far away as Hong Kong and as near as the UK and France are all sent to the right manufacturing plants in the UK, Northern Europe and India, using EDI. Recently, we have successfully implemented an international payments system via Citibank, and in the UK we make almost all our payments to suppliers and staff through the BACS service.

So we use EDI to address our key trading needs - and this use is expanding into the use of new EDI messages and applications for invoicing and blanket ordering.

4.3 Electronic mail speeds action

ICL first started using electronic mail in 1982, with some 200 select people on QUIKCOMM/DIALCOM. The E-mail strategy was defined in 1983 after this initial pilot and by 1984 we had almost 2,500 people using our own proprietary system. It was soon recognised that we needed a more "open" approach for E-mail and by 1988, had initiated our pilot X.400 service. Now, 26000 ICLers world-wide converse with their counterparts in sales, marketing, production, development and headquarters units, using X.400 compliant mail services and our proprietary systems have almost vanished.

Not only is this vital for internal working within and between countries, across timezones and with a fairly mobile workforce - over 350 major suppliers and clients are also linked into the system. This far-reaching service allows great synergy between co-operating units inside and outside ICL

- forecasting is made more slick, with full documentation available to headquarters planners within minutes of finalisation in outlying operational units.
- product developers and suppliers can discuss engineering requirements and schedules, with drafts being passed back and forth for refinement without the need for so many costly and time-consuming face-to-face meetings and site visits.
- memos, proposals, reports, plans, contracts, initial orders - all can be prepared where the specialists are and then sent rapidly through the service. For example, a specialist sales proposal prepared in the UK and France can be delivered within 1/2 hour to clients in Australia ready for their start of day, locally edited if appropriate, and printed on ICL Australia's note paper.

4.4 Concurrent and Remote Engineering

By collaborating closely with our suppliers and starting to exploit the techniques of concurrent engineering, we have been able to shorten time-to-market even where the circuit designers and the component developers are far apart - sometimes on opposite sides of the world. We have over ten years experience of working like this, first and foremost with Fujitsu. We have demonstrated this capability more recently by launching a successful new range of Personal Computers only 6 months after we merged with Nokia Data - with the range being designed jointly in Finland and the UK.

Electronic mail and extensive use of video-conferencing, plus transfer of engineering development files based on international standards so that all parties can read and use the data - all these techniques underpin our moves into concurrent design, development and production. Once a product is delivered to a client, then many of the hardware items in a computer system can now be checked, and update or repair software applied, remotely over an electronic link. We are also supplying diagnostic information on CD-ROM to allow users much more easy and rapid access, and to reduce our post and carriage bills substantially (not to mention saving quite a few trees).

4.5 The Result

The result of these initiatives in ICL is

- dramatically shorter product development lead times - from years to months.
- product order lead times down from months to weeks or even days. PC despatches are now targeted at less than 48 hours, and are often being achieved well within 1 working day.
- a consequent easing of the forecasting burden, and help for those doing the forecasting through electronic transmission of reports and spreadsheets.

- much better relationships with key suppliers.
- higher quality products, based on a better understanding of clients' requirements by both ICL and, in turn, by our suppliers.
- much lower stocks of components and finished products.
- much more interactive and capable scheduling and briefing of specialists skilled in addressing specific client needs, leading to better sales proposals, better exploitation advice, and more useful help to our suppliers.
- much quicker and more effective repair capabilities for installed equipment and software.
- significant reduction in the costs of developing, ordering, producing, selling and after-sales operations.
- and, for all our clients and suppliers, a much more responsive ICL.

5. Where Next?

While ICL is already well advanced in the new age of electronic trading, there are still fresh areas to exploit. Firstly, there is the extension and roll out of these new and exciting business methods within our own operations and with our trading partners so that all can benefit. Secondly, there are completely new areas to address.

5.1 Extension and Roll out

We currently focus our EDI electronic trading on purchasing, using the EDIFICE Purchase Order Message set, Order Acknowledgements and Invoices. With our existing EDI partners we intend to extend the range of transactions to cover not only blanket orders and payments, but also the exchange of forecasts, quality statistics and quotations.

We are addressing the next phase of our roll out to reach a further

200-plus suppliers, backed by personal interest and involvement from Peter Bonfield, ICL's Chairman and Chief Executive. As a further stage, we are also starting to use "hybrid" technologies such as the Royal Mail's EDIPOST service in order to reach yet more of our smaller suppliers.

5.2 New Areas

Many of the benefits of concurrent engineering stem from better communication and team working. Plans are afoot to give suppliers improved E-mail access to ICL, and there is work proceeding on a Corporate Components Library to facilitate better component specification and selection during logical and physical design stages. We envisage suppliers sending ICL technical component data in IEC 617 format, and for this to be used to update the Component Library without any manual rekeying. Initial talks have begun with a small number of key suppliers - after implementation it is hoped to extend this facility to many more of our suppliers.

Use of the Library should mean we are able more efficiently to design circuits, and to predict better their operating characteristics - such as reliability. It should also mean more business and better business for our partners, with less hassle and fewer errors and misunderstandings. It forms one aspect of an increased interest in concurrent engineering, being taken up particularly in our Corporate Systems Division.

Another aspect is the transmission of engineering drawings over networks - already working on International Network Services' TRADANET service - allowing partners to send explanatory drawings along with their electronic orders. We are exploring the network facilities needed to exchange the larger CAD files, and the benefits this could give over exchange of physical magnetic media.

So much for ICL buying from its suppliers! We have not forgotten or ignored our customers though and we plan to provide an increasing number of customers (both end-users and Value Added Resellers) with better ICL product information and ways to select and order from us. These methods will exploit the same core electronic technologies of EDI and E-mail to further boost our already rising sales productivity. Indeed we are already issuing product descriptions to some customers via E-mail and have a dial-up system configuration service that despatches the resultant details also via E-mail.

Subsequent delivery of software and services will where possible also be effected electronically. Internally, we already issue 'fix on fail' software upgrades world-wide via X.400, with attachments describing what is being sent and how to install it - some may even by installed automatically.

6. The Payoff - Summary

In the fiercely competitive global IT market, it is essential that we are always striving to do business Better, Faster and Cheaper. ICL, as a leading international player, is exploiting electronic trading techniques to achieve these goals and thus deliver competitive advantage for ourselves and our trading partners. We already have firm proof of benefits in lead times, reduction in errors, reduction in costs - accruing to our business partners as well as to ourselves. We have also extended our business to areas that would not have been possible without ET:-

- INS is our joint venture company set up with GEIS to run the UK EDI service TRADANET.
- we have expanded ICL's core product business to include fast moving commodity items (UNIX and PCs) where delivery lead times are measured in hours and enhanced these with a full range of software products and added-value services.

All in all, a worthwhile move to have made!

D Glossary

A

ACTM	Advanced Concept Technical Manual
AFNOR	French standards institute
AGV	Automated Goods Vehicle
AIAC	(US) automotive industry X12 standards group
AIAG	(US) automobile industry action group
ALLEGRO	French EDI service
ALPHA	German customs system
ANA	Article Numbering Association
ANSI	American National Standards Institute
ANSI X.12	ANSI accredited standards committee X.12
APACS	(UK) Association for Payment and Clearing Services
API	Application Program Interface
APIA	API Association
ASCII	American Standard Code for Information Interchange
ASEB	Asian EDIFACT Board
AT&T EDI	AT&T's EDI VAN service
ATM	Automated Teller Machine **also**: Asynchronous Transfer Mode
AUSTRIAPRO	Austria's Trade Facilitation Board
AWB	AirWay Bill

B

BABT	British Approvals Board for Telecommunication
BACS	(UK) Bankers Automated Clearing System
BAI	Bankers Automated Interface (for BACS)

Bankline	National Westminster Bank's EDI service
BDI	Business Data Interchange (ANSI X12)
BEDIS	Book trade Electronic Data Interchange Standard
BPR	Business Process Reengineering or Redesign
BSC	Binary Synchronous Communication (IBM)
BSI	British Standards Institute
BT	British Telecommunications
BT-GOLD	BT's X.400 service
BUKA	Austria's ANA

C

CAC	Computer Aided Chaos
CAD	Computer Aided Design
CADDIA	European project Co-operation in Automation of Data and Documentation for Imports/Exports and Agriculture
CAE	Computer Aided Engineering
CALS	Computer-aided Acquisition and Logistics Support (US Defense Department's ET programme)
CAM	Computer Automated Manufacture
CAPP	Computer Aided Process Planning
CASE	Computer Aided System Engineering
CAST	Computer Aided System Testing
CBT	Computer Based Training
CCC	Customs Co-operation Council
CCITT	International Consultative Committee for Telephony and Telegraphy (an agency of the ITU)
CD+G	Compact Disc + Graphics
CD-DA	Compact Disc Digital Audio
CD-I	Compact Disc Interactive
CD-R	Compact Disc Recordable
CD-ROM	Compact Disc Read Only Memory

CD-ROM XA	Compact Disc Read Only Memory Extended Architecture
CDIF	CASE Data Interchange Format (US Electronic Industries Association's CASE standard)
CDPD	Cellular Digital Packet Data
CDTV	Commodore Dynamic Total Vision
CE	Concurrent Engineering
CEC	Commission of European Communities **also** - Chinese EDI co-ordinating group
CEFIC	Confederation of European Chemical Industries PEG
CEN	The European Commission for Standardisation
CETS	(Hong Kong) Community Electronic Trading Service
CGM	Computer Graphics Metafile
CHAPS	(UK) Clearing House Automated Payment System
CHIEF	(UK) Customs Handling of Import and Export Freight (replaces Departmental Entry Processing System [DEPS])
CIDX	(US) Chemical industry X.12 standards group
CIM	Computer Integrated Manufacturing
CITIS	Contractor Integrated Technical Information Services (CALS)
CLI	Calling Line Identification **also**: Call Level Interface (SQLAG)
CM	Configuration Management
CMC	Common Messaging Call - a cross platform API
CMIP	Common Management Information (OSI system management protocol)
COLD	Computer Output to Laser Disc
COMPAT	(European) COMPuter Aided Trade - annual conference
Compression	Method of reducing images
COMPRO	The Community grouping of the national trade facilitation organisations of each country

CORBA	Common Object Request Broker (OMG)
COSTPRO	Canada's Trade Facilitation Board

D

DANPRO	Denmark's Trade Facilitation Board
DASS 2	Digital Access Signalling System 2
DAT	Digital Audio Tape
DCC	Digital Compact Disc
DCE	Distributed Computing Environment (the OSF's OTM standard)
DDI	Direct Dialling In
DEDIST	Swedish EDI promotion group
DEPS	(UK) Departmental Entry Process System (being replaced by CHIEF)
DEUPRO	Germany's Trade Facilitation Board
DIN	Germany's standards institute (equivalent to BSI,UK)
DIP	Document Image Processing
DISH	Data Interchange for Shipping
DME	Distributed Management Environment (the OSF system management standard)
DMS	Document Management System
DMTF	Desktop Management Task Force
DoD	(US) Department of Defense
DPNSS	Digital Private Network Signalling System
DSSSL	Document Style Semantics and Specification Language
DTD	Document Type Definition
DTI	(UK) Direct Trader Input to customs **also:** (UK) Department of Trade and Industry
DTP	Desktop Publishing **also**: Distributed Transaction Processing

E

EACOC	Spanish EDI service
EAN	International Article Numbering Association PEG
EANCOM	EAN's EDI project
EASAS	A working party for the Electrical Appliance Industry
Easylink	AT&T's EDI VAN service
EC	European Community (now European Union)
ECE	Economic Commission for Europe
ECIF	Electronic Component Industry Federation
ECMA	European Computer Manufacturers Association
ECR	Efficient Consumer Response (US equivalent of QR)
EDI	Electronic Data Interchange
EDI*EXPRESS	GEIS's EDI VAN service
EDI*NET	BT's EDI VAN service
EDIA	EDI Association originally set up by SITPRO (UK)
EDIAI	Ireland's EDI Association
EDIBUILD	EDI for the construction industry PEG
EDICA	Australian EDI Council
EDICIN	Construction industry EDI user group
EDICUG	(UK) Electronics industry EDI Components User Group
EDIF	Electronic Design Interchange Format
EDIFACT	EDI for Administration, Commerce and Transport
EDIFICAS	EDI for the accounting industry PEG
EDIFICE	EDI Forum for companies with Interests in Computing and Electronics PEG
EDIFORUM	Holland's EDI Association
EDIFRANCE	France's Trade Facilitation Board
EDIGRAC	Greek EDI awareness centre
EDIPAP	EDI paper industry PEG
EDIPOST	(UK) Royal Mail's EDI postal service

EDIS	Swedish EDI Association
EDISHIP	(UK) EDI user group for the shipping industry
EDITEXT	EDI textile industry PEG
EDIVIN	EDI wine industry PEG
EDM	Engineering Data Management
EEMA	European Electronic Mail Association
EEO	European Express Organisation PEG
EFT	Electronic Funds Transfer
EFTA	European Free Trade Association
EFTPOS	Electronic Funds Transfer at Point Of Sale
EIDX	(US) electronics industry X12 standards group
EIRPRO	Ireland's (Eire) Trade Facilitation Board
EIS	Executive Information System
E-mail	Electronic Mail
EMA	(US) Electronic Mail Association
EMEDI	EDI healthcare industry PEG
EMX	Enterprise Mail Exchange (SoftSwitch)
ENS	European Nervous System - telecommunications for administration
EOLAS	Ireland's Trade Facilitation Board
EPOS	Electronic Point Of Sale
ERP	Enterprise Resource Planning (MRP II +)
ESPRIT	European Strategic Programme of Research and development of Information Technology
ET	Electronic Trading
ETSI	European Telecommunications Standards Institute

F

FACTnet	Mongolian Network of Finance, Administrative, Commerce and Transport Telecommunications Network
FASTRAK	(UK) Midland Bank's VADS

FAX	Facsimile transmission
FCIM	(US) Army Flexible Computer Integrated Manufacturing
FDDI	Fibre Distributed Data Interface
FEDI	Financial EDI
FINPRO	Finland's Trade Facilitation Board
FIPS	(US) Federal Information Processing Standards
FOSI	Format Output Specification Instance
Frame	A block of data on compact disc
Frame Grabber	A device which converts image into digital data
FTAM	File Transfer, Access and Management

G

GDN	(UK) Government Data Network
GEDIS	India's Gateway for EDI Service
GEIS	General Electric Information Services (EDI*EXPRESS operators)
GEMS 400	India's Gateway Electronic Mail Service
GIS	Geographical Information System
GOSIP	(UK) Government OSI Profile
Group IV	International Standard for raster graphics
GTDI	Guidelines on Trade Data Interchange (strictly UN-GTDI now merging with EEMA)
GUI	Graphical User Interface

H

HCI	Human Computer Interaction
HUNPRO	Hungary's Trade Facilitation Board

I

I-EDI	Interactive EDI
IATA	International Air Transport Association

IBM	International Business Machines
ICARUS	Irish Community Air cargo Realtime Users System
ICC	International Chamber of Commerce
ICEPRO	Iceland's Trade Facilitation Board
ICL	International Computers Ltd
ICR	Intelligent Character Recognition
IDA	European programme for Interchange of Data between Administrations
IDAPI	Integrated Database Application Programming Interface (an SQLAG CLI)
IDEA	International Data Exchange Association
IDEF	Integrated Computer Aided Manufacturing Definition Language
IDX	European Interbank Data eXchange settlement service
IEEE	Institute of Electrical and Electronic Engineers
IETF	Internet Engineering Task Force
IETM	Interactive Electronic Technical manual
IFTM	International Forwarding and Transportation Messages
IGES	Initial Graphics Exchange Specification (an ANSI standard)
IMA	Interactive Multimedia Association
IN	Intelligent Network **also** Information Network, IBM's VAN
INET	Irish National Electronic Trading Network
INS	International Network Services (TRADANET operators) an ICL/GEIS Joint Venture
INTRASTAT	European cross border statistical return
IPD	Integrated Product Development
IPS	Institute of Purchasing and Supply
IPSS	International Packet Switching Service

IRDS	Information Resource Dictionary System (family of CASE standards)
ISDN	Integrated Services Digital Network
ISO	International Standards Institute
ISO 7372	Trade Data Element Directory standard
ISO 9735	UN/EDIFACT syntax standard
ISO 9796	Standard for Digital Signatures
ISPBX	Integrated Service Private Branch Exchange
ITU	International Telecommunications Union
IVHS	(US) Intelligent Vehicle Highway System
IWSDB	Integrated Weapon System Data Base (CALS)

J

JEDI	Joint EDI council (Europe & USA)
JEDIC	Japan's EDI Council
JEMA	Japan's Electronic Mail Association
JIBE	BP, Mobil and Shell's Joint Industry Billing Exchange project
JIT	Just In Time
JSEB	Japan / Singapore EDIFACT Board

K

KTNET	Korea Trade NETwork

L

L420	The CCITT ISDN basic rate standard
LACES	London Airport Cargo Export Scheme
LAN	Local Area Network
LAN Bridge	Method of connecting LAN to remote services
LaserDisc	Optical disc holding digital sound and analogue video

M

MAP	Manufacturing Automation Protocol
MAPI	Microsoft API
MasterPay	The Royal Bank of Scotland's EDI service
MDN	Managed Data Network
MessageWay	Logica's messaging service
MHS	Message Handling Service
MIB	Management Information Base (committee of MMCF)
MICR	Magnetic Ink Character Recognition
MIT90	Management In The Nineties Research Programme
MMCF	MultiMedia Communications Forum
MRP II	Manufacturing Resource Planning
MRP	Material Requirement Planning
MSN	Multiple Subscriber Number
MTA	(MHS) Message Transfer Agent
MTS	(MHS) Message Transfer Service

N

NCC	(UK) National Computer Centre
NCCL	National Commission for Communications Liberalisation
NCS	Network Control System
NET	EC standards body - "Normes Europeennes de Telecommunications"
NICK	Swedish project - Neutral Intelligent CAD Communication
NORPRO	Norway's Trade Facilitation Board
NT1	Network Termination 1 - PTT termination unit for ISDN

O

OCEAN	Ocean Carriers Electronic Access Network software
OCR	Optical Character Recognition
ODA	Open Document Architecture
ODBC	Open DataBase Connectivity (Microsoft)
ODETTE	Organisation for Data Exchange by Tele-Transmission in Europe - automotive industry PEG
OfficePower	ICL's integrated office system
Oftel	(UK) Office of Telecommunications
OFTP	The Odette File Transfer Protocol
OLTP	On-Line Transaction Processing
OMG	Object Management Group
ONP	European Open Network Provision policy
OPEN*framework*	ICL's Open Systems Architecture
OSF	Open Software Foundation
OSI	Open Systems Interconnection
OSLAN	Open System Local Area Network
OTM	Open Transaction Management

P

PAD	Packet Assemblers / Disassemblers (used in PSS)
PBX/PABX	Private Branch Exchange
PCI	Peripheral Component Interface
PCTE	Portable Common Tool Environment (European CASE standard)
PDA	Personal Digital Assistant
	also: Personal Data Assistant (Apple)
PDES	Product Data Exchange using STEP (CALS)
PDS	Premises Distribution System (AT&T)
PEG	Pan-European EDI Group
PEL	Picture Element (of raster graphics)

Photo CD	Digitising method for photographs
PIDX	(US) petroleum industry X12 standards group
PIPE	Paper Industry Pilot EDI project
Pixel	PEL on screen
POLPRO	Poland's Trade Facilitation Board
PortNet	Port of Singapore Authority system
POS	Point Of Sale
PostScript	Adobe's proprietary page description language standard for controlling laser printers and image setters
PROTECT	European ports project on dangerous drugs control
PSS	Packet Switching System (e.g. BT, Mercury, Transpac)
PSTN	Public Switched Telephone Network
PTO	Public Telecommunications Operator
PTT	Post, Telegraph and Telephone authorities
PUSHED	Practical Use of Software and Hardware in Exchanging Data

Q

QR	Quick Response (Retail's JIT)

R

RAMP	(US) Navy Rapid Acquisition of Manufactured Parts
RASTER	Scanned image
RDA	Remote Database Access (OSI system management protocol)
RINET	Re-insurance and Insurance NETwork PEG
RPC	Remote Procedure Call (OSI system management protocol)

S

SAD	Single Administration Document
SDH	Synchronous Digital Hierarchy (the European underlying transmission technology for ATM)
SDIF	SGML Data Interchange Format
SDLP	Synchronous Data Link communications protocol (IBM)
SEA	Single Europe Act
SEAGHA	Belgian ET project for port of Antwerp
SEDAS	Austria/Germany EDI standard for the retail industry
SEMPROITALIA	Italy's Trade Facilitation Board
SET	Standard d'Exchange et de Transfer France's Aerospatiale Corporation's equivalent of SGML
SGML	Standard Generalised Markup Language
SII	System Internal Interfaces
SIMPROESPANA	Spain's Trade Facilitation Board
SIPROCOM	Belgium's Trade Facilitation Board
SITA	Service Informatique Transports Aeronautiques
SITPRO	(UK) Simpler Trade Procedures Board
SITPRONETH	Holland's Trade Facilitation Board
SITPROSA	South Africa's Trade Facilitation Board
SKU	Stock Keeping Unit (retail)
SMDG	Shipping Message Development Group PEG
SME	Small & Medium Enterprises
SMMT	Society of Motor Manufacturers and Traders (maintain ODETTE standard)
SNA	System Network Architecture communications protocol (IBM)
SNMP	Simple Network Management Protocol (the Internet system management standard)
SNS	Singapore Network Services

Sonet	Synchronous Optical Network (the US underlying transmission technology for ATM)
SPARES	(US) Air Force Spare Part Production and Reprocurement System
SPDL	Standard Page Description Language
SPEED	Scottish Partnership in Electronic for Effective Distribution
SPI	System Programming Interfaces
SQL	Standard Query Language
SQLAG	SQL Access Group
STDL	Structured Transaction Definition Language (Digital Equipment Corporation's OTM standard)
STEDI	Hong Kong's Trade Facilitation Board
STEP	Standard for the Exchange of Product model data
STP	Shielded Twisted Pair
SWEPRO	Sweden's Trade Facilitation Board
SWIFT	Society for World-wide Interbank Financial Telecommunications PEG
SWISSPRO	Switzerland's Trade Facilitation Board
SWITCH	A debit card (electronic cheque)

T

TA	Telecommunications Administration
TCIF	(US) telecommunications industry X.12 standards group
TCO	Total Cost of Ownership
TCP/IP	Transmission Control Protocol / Internet Protocol
TDCC	(US) Transport Data Co-ordinating Committee
TDED	(UN) Trade Data Elements Directory (strictly UN-TDED)
TDI	Trade Data Interchange
	also: Technical Data Interchange

TEDIS	Trade Electronic Data Interchange System
TOP	Technical and Office Protocols
Touchscreen	Touch sensitive computer terminal
TQM	Total Quality Management
TRADACOMS	(UK) ANA EDI standard
TRADANET	INS's EDI VAN service
TRADE-VAN	Taiwan's project for cargo clearance automation
TRADEGATE	Australian communications network for the transport industry
TradeLink	Lloyds Bank's EDI service
TradeNet	Singapore government's network service
TradePay	Midland Bank's EDI service
Trading Master	Barclay's Bank EDI service
TRANSPOTEL	A provider of EDI services and standards for the European freighting industry & customs

U

UA	(MHS) User Agent
UCS	(US) grocery industry standards group
UKCEDIS	(UK) Confederation for EDI standards
UN-ECE	UN Economic Commission for Europe
UN-JEDI	UN Joint EDI project
UN-TDED	UN Trade Data Element Directory
UN-TDI	UN guide to Trade Data Interchange
UN-TDID	UN Trade Data Interchange Directory
UNCITRAL	UN Commission on International Trade Laws
UNSM	Universal Standard Messages (EDIFACT messages submitted to ISO)
UPS	Uninterruptible Power Supply
USPS	(US) Postal Service
UTP	Unshielded Twisted Pair

V

VADS	Value Added and Data Services
VAG	Volkswagen Audi Group
VAN	Value Added Network
VANGUARD	(UK) campaign to promote the use of VADS
VDA	VAG (German) EDI standard for automotive industry
VDA-FS	VDA's advanced form of IGES
Vector	Drawn image
VEDI	Dutch EDI programme
VICS	(US) retail industry standards group
VIM	Vendor Independent Messaging API (Lotus)

W

WAN	Wide Area Network
WE/EB	Western European EDIFACT Board
WINS	(US) Warehousing standards body

X

X.12	(US) ANSI standard for inter-industry EDI
X.25	International communications protocol for packet switching telecommunications
X.400	International message handling protocol for electronic mail and EDI
X.435	The Pedi syntax for transmission of EDI messages over an X400 network
X.500	The address directory for users of X400
X.509	CCITT recommendation for standard user authentication
X/Open	Consortium of IT suppliers established to adopt, promote and adapt open standards
XAPIA	X.400 API Association
XDS	X.500 Directory Service API
XPG	X/Open Portability Guide

Index

C

D

F

G

H

I

Q

R

S

W

X